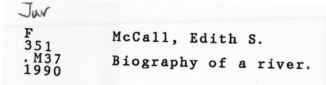

BIOGRAPHY OF A RIVER

THE LIVING MISSISSIPPI

BIOGRAPHY OF A RIVER: THE LIVING MISSISSIPPI

Edith McCall

Walker and Company ❋ New York

First published in the United States of America in 1990
by Walker Publishing Company, Inc.

Published simultaneously in Canada by Thomas Allen & Son
Canada, Limited, Markham, Ontario

Library of Congress Cataloging-in-Publication Data

McCall, Edith S.
Biography of a river: the Mississippi / by Edith McCall.
Summary: Traces the history of the Mississippi River, presents
stories of people whose lives are affected by the river, and
describes how humans have changed the Mississippi.
ISBN 0-8027-6914-4. —ISBN 0-8027-6915-2 (lib. bdg.)
1. Mississippi River—History—juvenile literature.
2. Mississippi River Valley—History—Juvenile literature.
[1. Mississippi River—History. 2. Mississippi River
Valley—History.] I. Title.
F351.M37 1990
977—dc20—89-70698
CIP

Printed in the United States of America

1 2 3 4 5 6 7 8 9 10

Book design by Shelli Rosen

To the rivers of North America, vital to American life today as they always have been.

ACKNOWLEDGMENTS

I thank Charles Kuralt for permission to quote from his article, "Down by the River," for the dedication page. Quinta Scott graciously furnished a copy of her unusual photograph of the Mississippi at St. Louis, featuring both the Eads Bridge and the Gateway Arch. To her and other photographers and artists who contributed to this book, I am grateful, including Putnam Museum of Davenport, Iowa, Minnesota's Itasca State Park, the Iowa Department of Transportation, Steve Golding of Ole Man River Towing, Vicksburg, and Dorothy Menard, who assisted in map preparation.

My research for *Biography of a River: The Living Mississippi* began years ago when I developed a lasting interest in river history. Various librarians have helped me locate source material, and I appreciate them and the many scholars whose published studies I've consulted through the years. For assistance with this book, I owe special thanks to Martin Reuss, Senior Civil Works Historian of the U.S. Army Corps of Engineers, as he furnished me with a wealth of material.

—EDITH McCALL
HOLLISTER, MISSOURI

"*Everything I love about America is a gift of the rivers: steamboats, pioneers, Huckleberry Finn, blue herons and snowy egrets, the Grand Canyon and the Blue Ridge hollows . . . jazz and catfish and ferryboats and covered bridges. None of them would be there, in memory or in fact, without the rivers. . . . America is a great story, and there is a river on every page of it.*"

—CHARLES KURALT

Contents

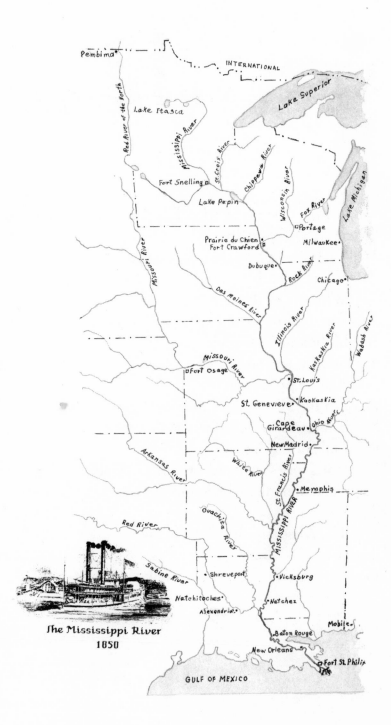

Pembima

INTERNATIONAL

Lake Superior

Red River of the North

Lake Itasca

Mississippi River

St. Croix River

Chippewa River

Wisconsin River

Lake Michigan

Fort Snelling

Lake Pepin

Fox River

Portage

Milwaukee

Missouri River

Prairie du Chien
Fort Crawford

Dubuque

Rock River

Chicago

Des Moines River

Illinois River

Kaskaskia River

Wabash River

Missouri River

Fort Osage

St. Louis

St. Genevieve

Kaskaskia

Cape
Girardeau

Ohio River

Arkansas River

New Madrid

White River

St. Francis River

Memphis

Ouachita River

Red River

MISSISSIPPI RIVER

Sabine River

Shreveport

Vicksburg

Natchitoches

Natchez

Alexandria

Mobile

Baton Rouge

New Orleans

Fort St. Philip

The Mississippi River
1850

GULF OF MEXICO

Meet Old Man River

Old Man River? That's what people call this ancient, yet ever new, river—the Mississippi. To those who live along or work on Old Man River, "he" seems to take on human qualities.

He's powerful, yet you can hold a bit of him in your hand, or gaze at his flowing waters and feel cooled and soothed.

He's deep and dark, and sometimes frightening; he's also sparkling, bright, and so clear you can see the bed on which he lies.

He's a friend, but he can also be an unpredictable enemy.

He flows between steep rocky bluffs, and he flows between land so flat and low that he sometimes spreads out and covers miles of it.

He has been the most important river in the story of the United States and possibly of all North America. He divides the land and yet he holds it together.

He's the marvelous Mississippi, and this is a true adventure story. It is the story of his life, of the people whose lives he affected, and of those who forced him to change. He's Old Man River, the Living Mississippi.

~~~~~~~~~~ The River Speaks

Old Man River! That's what people call me. And yes, I am old, for I have been flowing toward the seas since the last Ice Age, thousands of years ago. Like you, I was not always full-grown, as I am now. I started life very, very small. Unlike you, it took me thousands of years to become the size I am today.

Yes, I am very old, but I am still powerful. And I shall still be flowing on when all the people now alive have left this world. I am a child of the Age of Glaciers, shaped by the great ice sheets and by my own flowing waters.

Long ago, the huge rocks and boulders frozen in the underside of the glaciers acted like giant bulldozers, gouging out hollows and carrying the earth along as the glacier crept onward. When melting began, the hollows became lakes.

In Minnesota the glaciers formed 10,000 of those lakes. It is said that my beginning is in one of those lakes, Lake Itasca, a lake fed by melting snow, rains, and bubbling springs.

At the north end of the lake, clear waters pour over a rim of gray rocks, rocks worn smooth and silky with my flow. There I glide from the lake, falling only a few inches at the start. My water is clear and fresh, flowing on a bed of fine golden gravel, less than twenty feet across and sparkling in the sunshine.

My birthplace is marked with a log post which carries this message: HERE 1475 FEET ABOVE THE OCEAN THE MIGHTY MISSISSIPPI BEGINS TO FLOW ON ITS WINDING WAY 2552 MILES TO THE GULF OF MEXICO.

But do I really start here at Lake Itasca? Chambers Creek bubbles into the southwest end of the lake from Elk Lake, and brooks and rivulets flow into Elk Lake. The biggest brook comes from Little Elk Lake, farther south and no bigger than a farm pond. Little Elk Lake has no feeder streams large enough to be called creeks, so perhaps *that* is where I truly begin.

But wait. Just west of Lake Itasca is a north-south ridge, supporting a line of tall, dark pine trees silhouetted against the sky. This ridge is a divide. The streams flowing westward from it go into the Red River of the North, which flows to Canada, and eventually to Hudson Bay. The streams flowing down the east side of the divide find their way to me.

HERE 1475 FT
ABOVE
THE OCEAN
THE MIGHTY
MISSISSIPPI
BEGINS
TO FLOW
ON ITS
WINDING WAY
2552 MILES
TO THE
GULF
OF MEXICO

WHERE THE MISSISSIPPI FLOWS FROM LAKE ITASCA, MINNE- SOTA. Courtesy of Itasca State Park Interpretive Program

3

It has been said that perhaps I really begin where a crow sits on a pine branch right above the divide. Rain water dripping off his beak finds its way into the Red River, but the water off his tail comes to me, the great Mississippi River.

I am one of the most winding rivers in the world. I meander, turning this way and then that. If a rock bluff blocks my way, I take the easy route and flow alongside it. If the bluff bends, I bend with it. But when I flow against soft earth, I carry some along with me.

I start my meandering before I have gone one hundred yards from those rocks at the edge of Lake Itasca. Along my banks, thickets of yellow-green willows have grown, crowding against the tall dark pines of the forest. I am still a gentle stream as I complete that first loop, and no one would think it likely I'd become the great river I am.

Strangely, I begin my long southward journey by flowing to the north for about sixteen miles, until I find myself flowing right through Lake Bemidji. In that lake my direction changes. I leave the lake at its eastern side and travel eastward through a chain of little lakes until I come to Lake Winnibigoshish, an Indian word meaning "miserable, wretched, dirty water." The lake and I are so shallow here that when winds come they stir up the muddy bottom. Beyond the lake, my banks are so marshy that lots of wild rice grows, food for people and birds.

Now the slope of the land carries me southeastward, getting me set for my true direction, and my current becomes faster. I come to rock shelves and boulders in my bed, and my waters rush and fall so fast that people call them rapids. When I reach Grand Rapids, Minnesota, I go south, and then southeast for a long way.

In the old days, where Minneapolis is today, my waters poured over a sixteen-foot rock ledge, called the Falls of St. Anthony. I rushed on downhill, dropping eighty feet in a half mile. The Minnesota River from the west and the St. Croix River from the north join me below the falls. Finally, where La Crosse, Wisconsin, is today, I settle down to a southerly direction—mostly, that is.

I don't meander quite as much just below the Falls because of the craggy bluffs in which I've cut a canyon. But below La Crosse I can wander again. As I flow along, I am joined by many other rivers. The longest of them is the Missouri, which has traveled over 2,000 miles from a divide in the northwestern Rocky Mountains, carrying the melted snows from those faraway peaks and picking up mud from the Great Plains as it flows toward me. When the Missouri reaches my banks, its brown waters flow side by side with my clearer flow for several miles.

Now I am the "Mighty Mississippi!" But I become even mightier when the great flow of the Ohio River enters, between Illinois and Kentucky. The Ohio, a water highway from the Appalachian Mountains, isn't as long as the Missouri, but it carries more water. Just before the Ohio reaches me, it has been joined by the Tennessee and the Cumberland Rivers.

Many lesser streams flow into me along my journey— the Wisconsin, the Rock, the Des Moines, and the Illinois, all before the Missouri reaches me. Below the

Ohio's mouth, the White, the Arkansas, and the Red are the largest rivers to join me from the west. Each of these rivers is fed by countless smaller streams. Together we form the greatest river system in all the world! We gather water from 1,250,000 square miles of land, from the Rockies to the Appalachians, from Canada to the Gulf of Mexico!

As I approach the Gulf, I am carrying a great load of silt—fifty pounds of mud in every thousand cubic feet of water. My waters meet the Gulf current and my load settles. Over the centuries, I have built a delta, and I continue to build it even as you read this.

I am old, but still powerful. When I was younger, I could stop boats with my strong currents or wreck them on hidden rocks and buried tree trunks. My waters could flood the land or dwindle to a depth too shallow for boats. When I chose to cut a new channel, I could change my course.

I am not as wild and untamed as I was when I was younger, for people have found many ways to control me. They've been known to say, "Old Man River has found his master now for sure," as they did when the steamboat was invented. But then I play another of my tricks, and they know I am still the great Mississippi, *a living river!*

~~~~~~~~~~~~~~~~~~~~~~~~~~~~~~~~~~~~

1

Early People
on the Mississippi

Scientists have learned that the ancestors of the first people known to have lived near the Mississippi came to North America from Asia. During the Ice Age, when glaciers still formed a great ice cap over the northern part of the earth, there was a bridge of land where the Aleutian Islands and the Bering Strait are now, off the coast of Alaska.

The Asian families who made the crossing were hunters following herds of animals that skirted the glacier to find pasture. The people traveled slowly, perhaps spending a whole season or even several years in one camping place where the hunting was good. Their children grew up and had children themselves before the families had gone far into North America.

There was an open valley on the east side of the Rocky Mountains of Canada, and some tribes took that route southward, moving ahead of the winter snows. Some of these people went eastward into what is now the northern United States. Eventually some arrived in the land where the Mississippi River has its source.

How early these people arrived was a mystery until 1932, when roadbuilders near the river's source came across human bones in the silt of an ancient lakebed. Archaeologists examined the skeleton, and reported that it was a young girl who had lived and died at least 20,000 years ago. People may have come to the headwaters of the Mississippi River even earlier—perhaps before the Great River itself had begun to flow from Lake Itasca.

The people of about 19,000 years later left much more evidence of how they lived than those early settlers did. The Mississippi River people of about 1,000 A.D. are generally known as "Mound Builders." They piled earth in round heaps, in the shapes of animals, or in great squares. Some of their mounds can still be seen today. The mounds were sometimes built for religious purposes, sometimes as fortifications, and often for the burial of their dead.

Some of the burial mounds and many refuse heaps found in front of caves were opened by archaeologists. They found fishhooks and the bones of pike, catfish, sheepshead, and other river fish in the remains. Along the upper Mississippi near the headwaters, it is evident that the wild rice growing in the marshes was the principal grain of these ancient people. Many of them chose to build their villages of round-topped hide tent dwellings along the river, if there was not a cave as a ready-made shelter nearby.

It is known that the river served not only to supply food and shelter, but also as a long distance transportation route even then. Copper from the north has been found in mounds as far away as Ohio, taken there by boatmen of these ancient tribes.

The first people to get the idea for a boat to carry them on the water probably lived before the Mound Builders. They may have noticed that logs would float and move with the current. Perhaps one of them tried to ride a log, only to find it difficult to keep from rolling off. It is likely that early people tied two or more logs together with tough vine or root strands to create a raft. It is also possible that someone noticed how an insect rode a curled leaf down the river. Perhaps that was the inspiration that led them to hollow out large logs, making crude boats that would carry people and have room for cargo, too.

Besides the raft and the dugout canoe, the Mound Builders also developed another kind of boat, making use of the hides they acquired through hunting the plentiful bison. This was the bullboat, so named because the hide of a large bull bison was the covering.

For the framework of the bullboat, slender tree limbs (probably spruce because it was flexible and plentiful in the northern woods) were arranged like wheel spokes, and bent upward at the ends. The softened hide was stretched over the framework, and tied in place with sinew or leather strips. This bowl-shaped boat would carry more people and goods than a hollowed log.

Although it continued to be used on the rivers of the northwestern plains for many years, there were problems with the bullboat. It took great skill with a paddle to keep a round boat from simply spinning around, especially when the boatmen were fighting the current, to go up the river. At day's end, the boat had to be taken ashore, emptied of its cargo, and the hide rubbed with fat to prevent it from splitting as it dried.

The raft, a crude dugout canoe, and bullboat were probably the first types of boats on the Mississippi. Somewhat later, the people of the northern Mississippi valley learned to make a much better boat—the long, lightweight bark canoe. There were miles and miles of forests of evergreen trees mixed with the startlingly white-barked birch trees, and these people discovered that a birch tree's bark, cut from the tree in large sheets, could be used for a flexible, waterproof boat covering.

The boat skeleton was made with ribs and crossbars of the slender young spruce trees, and the cord-like roots of the same trees were used to tie the pieces together. The frame was pulled to a point at both ends, and then curved upward to form the closing. Roots were also used to stitch the birch-bark to the framework. Pitch from the yellow pine sealed the seams to make the canoe watertight. Paddles were usually cut from another of the northern evergreens, the white cedar.

By the time the Europeans arrived in the Mississippi valley, the Mound Builders with their advanced culture had disappeared, for reasons still not definitely known. The Mississippi River valley was now peopled by Indian tribes familiar to us. The earliest known of the Indians who lived along the upper Mississippi were the Dakotas of the Sioux family of tribes, and the Ojibwa of the Algonkian family. Because of the way the Europeans pronounced Ojibwa, these people came to be better known as the Chippewas.

The Sioux and Algonkian families of tribes were usually enemies, and they clashed in the lands around the Mississippi. The Dakotas had long occupied the northern part of Minnesota, but the Ojibwa were pushing into their lands from the northeast. In the battles between Chippewa and Dakota, the Dakotas were forced farther west. When white explorers arrived in the 1600s, the Chippewa were just beginning their drive into northeastern Minnesota. Dakotas were living in the woodlands of the headwaters of the Mississippi River.

Dakota villages were permanent groups of rounded

THE INDIAN CANOE WAS COPIED BY THE FRENCH FUR TRADERS TO TRAVEL THE RIVERS AND LAKES. From a painting by Frederic Remington

11

wigwams. The people dressed in deerskins and hunted with bows and arrows. The rivers were important to them, both to supply fish and as a means of transportation in a bullboat or canoe. Clam and oyster shells from the Mississippi were valued for making ornamental pieces and for use as scraping tools.

The Dakotas and later the Chippewas went by boat to the marshlands of the upper Mississippi to harvest the wild rice that grew there. They would gather a handful of the long ripened stems, bend them over the canoe framework and pound the stem so that the grain fell into the canoe.

Farther down the Mississippi was another tribe of the Sioux family, the Winnebago. Unlike most Sioux, they lived principally on the eastern side of the river in what is now Wisconsin. In Illinois on the east side of the Mississippi and Iowa on the west, there were other Algonkian tribes, the people of the Illinois Confederacy.

South of Illinois and Iowa, most of the west bank of the Mississippi was held by Sioux tribes and the east by Algonkian. In what would be southern Arkansas today, were the Quapaw of the Sioux family, and south of them, in Louisiana, the Sioux Caddo Confederacy. The Algonkian Shawnee, Chickasaw, Choctaw, and Natchez were on the eastern side.

Although the Algonkian and Sioux tribes often battled, they had much in common. None of them thought the land belonged to any one person, nor that the Mississippi was any tribe's property. It was a source of food and transportation for all.

But the white men from Europe were about to intrude into their world. They would come with their huge, noisy guns, their horses, and their steel breastplates no arrow could penetrate. Worst of all, they would bring their strange ideas of owning the land—and the Mississippi River.

2

White Men
Find the Mississippi

Hernando de Soto, Governor of Cuba under Spanish rule, raised his hand signalling the company of weary men behind him to stop. Seated on his war horse at the edge of a low bluff, De Soto looked down in amazement at the river beyond. Even partially hidden by thickets of willows along its bank, it was awesome! He judged it must be nearly two miles wide.

One of the captains gathered around him later wrote of this moment, ". . . a man could not be distinguished from one side to the other; it was very deep and very rapid, and being always full of trees and timber that was carried down by the force of the stream, the water was thick and very muddy." The river was the Mississippi, seen by white men for the first time on May 8, 1541, just below today's city of Memphis, Tennessee. The "trees and timber" they saw in the river were probably torn loose from the Mississippi's banks in the spring rains of that year.

One of the purposes of this exploring expedition, sent by the King of Spain, was to find a waterway to the Pacific Ocean. Could this be the river the explorers had been seeking?

De Soto named his discovery "Rio Grande," meaning Great River, not knowing how great a river the Mississippi truly was. Most of the men following De Soto were too tired to care much about this river. It had been two years since they had left Florida, some on horses but most on foot. Indian prisoners captured in many small battles brought up the rear of their long marching procession, carrying supplies on their backs. They had come through today's states of Florida, Georgia, Alabama, and Mississippi, forcing Indian chiefs in the villages they found to do as De Soto commanded.

In the holds of their ships, the Spanish had brought about 200 horses for the officers to ride, and hundreds of squealing pigs to supply meat to the men as they explored. Every Indian chief with whom they spoke was asked for gold. All said they had none, but that the "cities of gold" were not far away, and all pointed westward. Had De Soto only known it, when he was in northern Georgia he was not far from a place where some gold was found in 1828.

Indians of the villages De Soto attacked had never before seen a horse, and the big Spanish steeds frightened them. The sound of a gun firing added to their terror. Hogs also were unknown to the Indians, but when the

Spaniards allowed some of them to taste the roasted meat, they found it delicious.

The Indians were happy to see these intruders go on their way. However, sometimes they left only after a battle in which they shot down the Indians who tried to stand against them. The only pleasant reminder the Spaniards left behind for the Indians was an occasional hog that had escaped to run wild in the woods.

As De Soto looked down upon the great river, he was about at the state line between Tennessee and Mississippi. He declared the river and the land to be the property of "God and the King of Spain." In 1541, most of the New World was claimed by that faraway monarch who had never left Spain.

De Soto decided that this wide river must be crossed, for there was a possibility that Indians on the other side could direct him to "El Dorado," the land of gold. The soldiers and slaves were ordered to cut down pine trees in the nearby woodlands to build four rafts on which men and animals could cross the Mississippi a few at a time. While the weeks it took to do this work were passing, curious Quapaw Indians from the other side of the Mississippi came near in their war canoes, the hollowed trunks of huge trees. The Quapaw were often at war with the Indians on the east side of the Great River, and were very suspicious of the intruders. De Soto gave them gifts to keep them from attacking his men.

In the meantime, he began to doubt that the Mississippi could be the waterway to the Pacific, for it flowed generally southward, and he expected a river passage to flow to the west. And so when all of his men had been taken to the western bank—the first Europeans to cross the Mississippi—De Soto led the men and their animals northward a short way and then turned to the west, seeking the cities of gold the Quapaws told him were in that direction. The men left the river's level floodplain and traveled through the low hills, reaching today's northern Arkansas and possibly southern Missouri, where they found a wooded area of low mountains, today's Ozarks.

As he met with Indians along the way, De Soto wanted to make them afraid to attack him and his men. Using a mirror as his "magic," he convinced them he was some kind of god, the "Child of the Sun" who could not die. The Indians accepted this when the white men prayed for rain for them—and a summer storm arose!

Traveling the Ozark Mountains was difficult and, discouraged at last, De Soto turned southeastward. He decided to go to the Gulf of Mexico and build ships in which all who had not died of disease or other causes would sail back to Florida.

Lacking maps to guide them to the Gulf, they found themselves in present southern Arkansas. A fatal fever struck the despairing De Soto while they were camped along the river there. His men feared the Indians would kill them all if they discovered the "Child of the Sun" was not a god, but a mere man, now dead. Some of the captains wrapped their leader's body in a blanket, weighted it with rocks, and took it in a canoe to the middle of the Mississippi under cover of darkness. There they dropped De Soto's body overboard.

DeSoto's body was dropped into the river, in the dark of night. Drawing by James G. Teason

Then they hastily constructed crude ships and rafts. All available cloth and some broad leaves were fashioned into sails. They were weak from hunger, for their hogs had either been slaughtered or had escaped into the Arkansas hills to become the ancestors of the Arkansas "razorback." About forty horses were still alive. They loaded them onto a raft at the end of their little flotilla as they started down the river. Amid arrows fired at men and horses by the no longer awestruck Quapaws, they floated down the Mississippi.

So ended the first voyage of white men on the great Mississippi River. It would be nearly 150 years before Old Man River would again be traveled by Europeans.

The same year that De Soto first saw the wide Mississippi, a fleet of ten French sailing ships entered another great North America river, the St. Lawrence, far to the north. The Frenchmen on board the ships had the same dreams as the Spanish—to find riches and a river passage through North America to the Pacific Ocean. They called this hoped-for river the "Northwest Passage." Ignoring the Spanish claim to all of North America, the French claimed it to be the property of "God and the King of France" and named the land New France.

In 1541, while De Soto was in Arkansas, Jacques Cartier, leader of the French expedition, was on the St. Lawrence for the third time. He hoped to start a colony at Quebec so that he could remain through the cold winter months and have time to explore a tributary—a river flowing into the St. Lawrence—now known as the Ottawa River. Cartier hoped that the Ottawa was the Northwest Passage they were seeking. But Cartier's men refused to stay in that wild, cold land, and he was forced to give up his dream. Had he been able to continue his explorations, he might well have learned of the Mississippi from the Indians of the Algonkian tribes of those northlands.

The King of France was busy with European wars at the time Cartier gave up his explorations, and sent no more explorers until 1608, when Samuel Champlain went up the St. Lawrence. He succeeded where Cartier had failed, establishing a base colony at Quebec from which to explore. More and more French came thereafter to New France and explorations continued, not only up the Ottawa but all around the northern Great Lakes.

The French discovered no gold, but they found another kind of "riches" with which to pay the costs of the expeditions. They made friends with the Algonkian Indians by trading European cloth and trinkets for the fine fur pelts that the Indians could bring them. The furs brought a good price in Europe.

Among the Algonkians the French met on their trading expeditions were the Chippewas who knew of a river they called the "Mesipi," an Indian name for "Great River." Perhaps, the French thought, this would be the river they sought—the waterway through North America!

They learned something else of great importance from the Indians—how to make birch bark canoes in which to travel the many shallow streams and the lakes of North America. The French also learned how the Indians moved from the headwaters of one river across land to the nearest stream to continue their journey. The birch bark canoes were so lightweight that they could be turned over and carried across the land by two men while others carried the cargo. Soon the French fur traders were building their own canoes to replace the heavy dugouts they had been using. They gave the French name *portage* to the land crossings from the word *porter*, which means "to carry."

In time, the French fur traders were building canoes thirty-five feet long and six feet wide at the middle. They used them on long voyages to take supplies to trading posts. For seats in the large canoes, they hung boards from the gunwales, short enough not to push against the fragile bark covering. Each large canoe could carry eight men, about 3,000 pounds of baggage, and supplies for keeping the canoe in good repair. During the land crossings, four men could portage the canoe, while the baggage was divided among the other four.

Traveling in that manner, a French fur trader-explorer, Jean Nicolet, while seeking the Northwest Passage, found the Straits of Mackinac where Lake Huron meets Lake Michigan. He traveled on Lake Michigan to Green Bay in 1634 and established the first trading post in what would become Wisconsin.

Many Catholic priests came to New France, not for riches but to teach the Indians of Christianity. Among them was Father Jacques Marquette, eager to find Indians who had never heard of Jesus. He was sent with an educated young man who also was experienced in frontier travel in New France, Louis Joliet, who intended to find and explore the Great River.

Marquette and Joliet left the Straits of Mackinac on May 15, 1673, with two small birch bark canoes and five of the French-Canadians known as *voyageurs*, the French name for traveling fur traders. Included in their supplies was a small portable altar for Father Marquette to use when converting Indians to Christianity. The priest was not expected to do any other work, such as paddling or portaging.

In spite of warnings from their Indian friends of monsters and all sorts of dangers lurking on the "Mesipi," Marquette and Joliet headed for the great unknown. They went to Green Bay and entered Fox River. Where the city of Portage, Wisconsin, is today, they portaged to a feeder stream of the Wisconsin River, a tributary of the Mississippi. They were on their way to the Great River!

21

On June 17 they saw before them a rocky bluff rising above the water beyond some islands. They knew this must be the west bank of the famed Mississippi, the "Big River" of which the Indians spoke. Just as they turned to start down the Mississippi, they felt something bump and nearly overturn the lead canoe. Could the Indians have been right about "monsters" in the river? Their "monster," probably a huge catfish, fortunately swam away and they regained control of their craft.

When they had recovered from their fright and could look around, the travelers were amazed to see the high wooded bluffs continue on their right, mile after mile. On the left was rolling woodland, where they could tie up at night and go on shore long enough to cook a meal. At night, fearing the wild animals, they slept as best they could in the canoes, with one man on guard duty.

The river wound this way and that, continuing the meandering that had been its habit from its beginning. After a week, when the Frenchmen found lower bluffs on the right bank, Father Marquette decided it was time to begin his work. He and Joliet followed a trail ashore, looking for an Indian village.

Fortunately, word had spread among the Indians of the peaceful "black robes." Four or five miles inland Marquette and Joliet were met by a greeting procession from a nearby village. The chieftain was carrying a calumet, the ceremonial peace pipe, and welcomed them. When they left the next day, their gifts included a three foot long calumet and an Indian boy who was to be their slave.

As they went on down the Mississippi, they saw huge red, black, and green paintings of strange creatures on the rock cliffs, so high above the river that the Frenchmen wondered how the artists had been able to do their work. When they passed the mouth of the Missouri River and met the discharge of tangled tree limbs, they thought of the warning they'd had of "a demon that could swallow canoes." The Chain of Rocks rapids a little farther downstream swept their canoes along much too fast for comfort, and they again feared being "swallowed," canoes and all.

The voyageurs, experienced in handling canoes on the northern rivers, kept them afloat, and eventually they passed the mouth of the Ohio River on their left. They continued downstream about as far as the place where De Soto's body had been given its river-bottom grave. Joliet began to worry that they might meet Spaniards who would take them as prisoners. He considered turning back.

Near the mouth of the St. Francis River in Arkansas, the explorers met a band of Quapaw Indians in dugout canoes who were in a most unfriendly mood. All that saved the Frenchmen was the calumet Joliet held aloft. That peace sign stopped the attack and made a conversation possible. The Quapaws told Joliet and Marquette that ten days' journey to the south was the "great sea," and possibly some Spaniards—an enemy they held in common.

The canoes were turned about for the much more difficult upstream voyage. When the explorers met the friendly

Illinois Indians again, they were directed to the Illinois River as a shorter route back to Lake Michigan. They followed it and portaged to the south end of the lake, arriving there at the end of September.

Marquette and Joliet had much information to add to their maps from their pioneering voyage on the Mississippi and two of its important tributaries, the Wisconsin and the Illinois. Joliet had been keeping records and drawing maps as they traveled. Unfortunately, as he was returning to Montreal with the Indian boy the next spring, his canoe overturned in some rapids. The Indian boy drowned and the records and maps were lost. Nevertheless, this first long journey down the great river added much to the store of knowledge about Old Man River.

3

Who Owns
the Great River?

More Frenchmen came to the St. Lawrence River valley each year. Some were farmers and tradespeople, but many were fur-traders and priests. For all, the rivers were the best routes and the French became as expert at building and using birch bark canoes as the Indians were.

Among the new arrivals from France in 1666 was Robert Cavalier de La Salle, the 23-year-old son of a well-to-do French family. La Salle had been educated in France by the Jesuit priests, but he was too restless to follow the Jesuits' strict rules and wanted a more adventurous life. He knew where to find it—in the wild lands across the Atlantic Ocean. As soon as he arrived, he purchased an estate at Lachine, near Montreal. There he built a fort, cleared land, brought in settlers, and opened a fur-trading post.

But this didn't satisfy his restless soul for long. He was a man with imagination and ambition. He thought of the many miles of unexplored land that lay to the south. How wonderful if all that land and the great seas and rivers the Indians spoke of could become part of New France! He, Robert Cavalier de La Salle, could be the man to help France build a huge empire in America.

In 1669, after only three years in America, he sold his land and took action to make his dream a reality. He began by getting approval for an expedition from the New France governor, and soon had hired men to go with him to Lake Ontario and beyond. Encounters with unfriendly Iroquois tribesmen on the south shore of Lake Ontario frightened his men, and when La Salle would not return to the safety of Montreal they deserted him.

Alone, he headed southward, learning day by day how to survive in the wilderness. He encountered more Iroquois and somehow made them believe he came as a friend. Eventually, he reached the Ohio River, the first Frenchman to do so.

When La Salle arrived back in Montreal after three years, he was greeted as someone back from the dead. He had not forgotten his dream to expand the French Empire and now planned to establish a chain of small forts along the Mississippi for defense of France's claims to the valley lands. The final fort would be at the mouth of the great river, and he would be the one to claim for France all the land the Mississippi River and its tributaries drained. He'd need men for the expeditions and to build and man the forts—financing from the French royal court was necessary. He set sail for France.

His proposal to reimburse the royal treasury with shipments of furs was approved. Soon he was back in New France, where he built the *Griffin*, the first sailing vessel on any of the Great Lakes. He built his ship at the east end of Lake Erie, near the Niagara River but above the falls. When it was finished he sailed it westward through Lakes Erie and Huron, into Lake Michigan and to Green Bay, where it took on a cargo of furs. While La Salle began his explorations, the furs were to be taken back to Niagara Falls and there transferred to Lake Ontario and the St. Lawrence River for shipment to France.

Young La Salle had one misfortune after another. He left Green Bay with four canoes and fourteen men, heading for the portage to the Illinois River. This move began years of struggle and unexpected disasters. His first great blow was the news that the *Griffin* had not reached Fort Niagara. Her cargo was lost and so there would be no funding arriving. But La Salle would not give up.

Only one man shared La Salle's dream of a New France from the mouth of the St. Lawrence to the mouth of the Mississippi. This man was Henry de Tonti, who had returned with La Salle from one of his journeys back to Europe. Tonti was an Italian war veteran with a steel claw to replace a hand he had lost in battle.

As the years passed and La Salle faced defeats, desertion, and even attempts on his life by his own soldiers, "Tonti of the Iron Hand" was the one man on whom La Salle relied. Terrible winters in the open, so little food that the men nearly starved, battles with Indians—nothing stopped La Salle and Tonti. Besides the forts and trading posts they built near the Great Lakes, they also erected the first log buildings along the Mississippi River, Forts Chartres and Kaskaskia in today's Illinois, about seventy-five miles above the Ohio River mouth.

Finally, after years of struggle and narrow escapes from death, La Salle, Tonti, and a small company of men completed a journey all the way down the Mississippi. After making their way through an arm of the river's great delta, they saw the Gulf of Mexico ahead. The men assembled for a ceremony on the riverbank on April 19, 1682. Standing beside a column cut from a tree on which was carved the name of King Louis XIV of France and the date, and holding the French flag and a wooden cross, La

LaSalle traveled via Indian canoe to explore the Mis-SISSIPPI. Drawing by Darrell Wiskur, for *Forts in the Wilderness*, Childrens Press

Salle claimed all the land drained by the Mississippi River system for "God and the King of France." He named the land "Louisiana." This meant that besides the St. Lawrence River and Great Lakes area, France claimed to own a great part of the land from the Rocky Mountains to the Appalachian Mountains and south to the Gulf of Mexico, for the Mississippi River system drained all that land.

Back in France, two years later, La Salle was given a fleet of four ships to carry soldiers and settlers to form a colony near the mouth of the Mississippi. It was to be a shipping center that would not be ice-blocked in winter as the St. Lawrence was. The ships set sail with the optimistic colonists in July, 1684.

The mouth of the Mississippi was then difficult to find from the Gulf of Mexico because the land was flat and marshy, looking much the same for miles. The river divided into three main channels and many small streams, but none were easily distinguished in the tall grasses of the marshy delta. The ships went a long distance before La Salle realized he had missed the river mouth. When the people who intended to build a city where New Orleans is now finally went ashore late in December, they had gone 400 miles too far and were halfway down the Texas coast.

It would be fine to be able to put a happy ending to the story of this great and adventurous explorer, but that was not to be. The landing in Texas was a disaster, as were the days that followed when the frustrated colonists tried to build crude shelters. The story of all that went wrong

29

is too long to tell here, but it includes wrecking the ships and loss of property, enemy attacks, terrible weather, and hunger. While trying to find the way back to the Mississippi in March, 1687, La Salle was murdered by one of his own men in the Texas wilderness.

Thirty-one years later, in 1718, La Salle's dream of a colony at the mouth of the Mississippi was realized. The French need for a shipping outlet there was greater than ever. The Governor of Louisiana was a French-Canadian named Sieur de Bienville. He had been building more forts along the Mississippi, and he found a site on a curve of the river not too far from its mouth that he thought would be protected from hurricanes and tidal waves. There men laid out streets where the French Quarter of New Orleans is now, and built huts for the expected colonists. Soon it was the hoped-for port where river boats met ocean ships.

After La Salle's explorations, the French considered the Ohio and Mississippi Rivers to be part of their vast colonial empire. Besides continuing to trade for furs the Indians brought to them, they found another source of income in what is now southeastern Missouri. They discovered lead that could be mined there and built furnaces for smelting. The lead was molded into the shape of horse collars and carried by horses to the riverbank. The first town in Missouri, Ste. Genevieve, was begun in 1735 as a shipping point to send the lead down to New Orleans.

In the meantime, Spain continued to claim the Mississippi River, as well as all the lands to the south and west, including part of Louisiana. Spain also claimed Florida and the land bordering the Gulf of Mexico. But a third nation, England, was also making land claims in North America. Trouble was brewing as claims overlapped.

Beginning in 1607, England had been building a colonial empire in America. The English colonists lived along the Atlantic coast, but claimed land far beyond the Appalachians. English maps and French maps showed overlapping claims, especially in the Ohio River valley.

Not very many people lived in the part of North America the Spanish claimed, except along the Mississippi River. But more and more people came from Europe to live in New France and in the English colonies. Since both France and England claimed to own the same land, they were bound to clash. And clash they did when the English began to push into the land between the Appalachian Mountains and the Mississippi River, claiming it was theirs to settle.

The Indians, of course, were sure it belonged to neither of these countries from across the ocean. To them all land belonged to the "Great Spirit." They sided more with the French, however, mostly because the French paid them for furs they brought from the wilderness and were willing to let them continue to have their villages. The English settlers insisted that most of the Indians must move on westward, out of their settled lands.

The clash came in the form of the French and Indian War, fought between 1754 and 1763. In the peace treaty that ended the war, France was the loser. Because of wars going on in Europe at the same time, Spain was also involved in the treaty. Great Britain was given the French claims in Canada and south of the Great Lakes as far west as the Mississippi River. Spain received all the rest of French "Louisiana," and gave up Florida to Great Britain.

While Great Britain and France were fighting, the French began a trading post village where pelts from up the Missouri River as well as those from the upper Mississippi could be handled for shipping. A site was chosen on a low bluff on the west bank of the Mississippi, just below the mouth of the Missouri River, where the city of St. Louis, Missouri, is today.

The first log buildings of St. Louis went up in 1764, built under the direction of Pierre Laclede and his fourteen-year-old clerk, Auguste Chouteau. They didn't know that the land on which they were building had just become Spanish property, but even after some Spanish officials arrived, they and other French settlers stayed on.

Old Man River flowed on between English lands to the east and Spanish lands to the west. Both sides considered the great old river as their own. But Spain had the advantage, since in the treaty a small strip of eastern land came with the Spanish "package"—land along the Gulf of Mexico coast all the way to Florida. That land included the port city of New Orleans.

After the United States became an independent nation in 1776, the Mississippi grew in importance. The peace treaty that ended the Revolutionary War in 1783 gave the land south of the Great Lakes and westward to the Mississippi to the United States of America, a young nation not yet grown to the strength of its old European founders.

Americans assumed the rivers belonged to them along with the land. But where did the rivers lead? To New Orleans, the port where goods could be transferred to sailing ships—which the Spanish controlled. American diplomats had to arrange an agreement with the Spanish to keep the port open so that western Americans were not cut off from shipping.

Now Old Man River had company much of the time. Boxy flatboats, like rafts with built up sides and perhaps a roof over part of the deck to protect the cargo, were poled down the Ohio to the Great River, carrying the products of the newly cleared fields of pioneer America. The corn and other products that the frontier farmers didn't need were wanted in the eastern cities, and it was less expensive to ship the long way by water than the shorter route over the Appalachian Mountains.

There were barrels of hams and bacon from the hogs that fed in the woods and flour from the grain that was grown. After a while there were also barrels of salt, cider, vinegar, whiskey, apples, and bundles of rope hemp. At New Orleans, the products were sold and transferred to sailing ships that would take them to the cities. The flatboat itself was broken into lumber and sold. Not even a crew of strong men could move a flatboat very far up the Mississippi River against the currents.

There was another kind of boat that also brought goods down to New Orleans and could be taken upriver with

KEELBOATMEN FIGHT THE MISSISSIPPI'S CURRENT AND SNAGS.
Drawing by Lloyd Hawthorne

some of the things the people of the American "West" needed. This was the keelboat, a long, slender boat with pointed ends, built on ribs rising from a keel, the long beam that ran under the center of the boat from end to end.

The keelboat had no power except that of husky boatmen's muscles. When it was loaded with goods brought to New Orleans by sailing ship, it took a powerful crew to pole the boat against the current. Often they had to go ashore and drag it upriver with the long rope called by the French name, *cordelle*. The river was sometimes more powerful than the whole crew, and the men would have to tie the cordelle around a sturdy tree near the bank. Then, on board the boat, the rope would be wound on a windlass to make the boat move forward. This was called warping.

By 1800, the question of who owned the Mississippi needed to be answered as more people came to depend on it. The Americans took it for granted that they could use the river freely, but the Spanish owners of Louisiana, including the city of New Orleans, did not agree and threatened to block American shipping. Old Man River was too important to Americans to allow that to happen!

4

The River
Becomes All-American

President Thomas Jefferson faced a great problem. He paced the floor in the drafty halls of the unfinished "President's House," trying to decide what to do. Every day another letter arrived from the West, and each time he met a congressman from either of the two western states— Kentucky or Tennessee—he was asked, "When? When are you going to get Spain to give the boatmen the 'right of deposit' again?"

He knew how much they needed this right, taken from them by Spain in October, 1802. It was the right to unload goods from their boats in New Orleans to be transferred to ocean sailing ships, and for American sailing ships to unload goods to be carried back up the Mississippi River.

There was little President Jefferson could do to influence those European rulers—they were at war with each other and too busy to listen to American matters. The United States was still an infant among nations in 1803, and some thought the new nation wouldn't last long. President Jefferson assured the congressmen that he knew open shipping on the Mississippi was important for the people west of the Appalachians—and there were more and more people there each year. Ohio was preparing to become a state, and people were flocking as far west as the Mississippi River. Some, like Daniel Boone, had even crossed the Mississippi into Spanish lands!

Then the President heard more startling news—Spain was about to turn Louisiana over to Napoleon Bonaparte, that upstart who had made himself dictator of France! Napoleon's French armies had already conquered Italy, Austria, and even Egypt. Jefferson immediately sent American representatives to Paris to make an offer to buy the river mouth area.

The timing was right. When the next dispatch came, the news was good. Napoleon was running out of money and wanted to build up his forces to attack England. He agreed not only to sell the land near the mouth of the Mississippi to the United States, but all the rest of Louisiana that La Salle had claimed for France.

For about fifteen million dollars, the United States could buy all the land west of the Mississippi drained by rivers that flowed into the Mississippi system. This huge area—about 829,000 square miles—was almost as large as the whole United States east of the Mississippi! President Jefferson sent the "go ahead" back by the fastest sailing ship.

The treaty was signed in Paris in May of 1803. The new American land was known as the Louisiana Purchase. Suddenly, the United States was sole owner of a huge wedge of land that reached to the Rocky Mountains. But most important to the people, the Americans now owned the Mississippi River!

In St. Louis, in the spring of 1804, boats were prepared for explorations in the Louisiana Territory. Like a person with a gift package, President Jefferson wanted to know what was inside this unexplored land. He knew a little about the lower Missouri River, but there was only hearsay about the upper river and how near its source was to the Pacific.

Neither did the President know much about the upper Mississippi. He had heard of the Falls of St. Anthony through the writings of one of the French missionaries, Father Hennepin. But very little was known about the Mississippi above the mouth of the Wisconsin River.

Expeditions would have several purposes: to map the great rivers, to let the Indians know of their new status under the "Great White Father" who would protect them, and to learn about the land's natural treasures of minerals and wildlife. Captain Meriwether Lewis, President Jefferson's secretary, and Lieutenant William Clark set out in May, 1804, to explore the Missouri River. Their travels are now know as the Lewis and Clark Expedition.

To explore the upper Mississippi, Jefferson left the choice of leaders to General James Wilkinson in St.

FALLS OF ST. ANTHONY, AS THEY APPEARED IN 1767. From a painting by explorer Jonathan Carver

Louis, who was in charge of the western armies and was also Governor of Upper Louisiana. His choice was Lieutenant Zebulon Montgomery Pike, the officer in charge of the old French fort of Kaskaskia on the Illinois side of the Mississippi.

Lieutenant Pike was bored with his duties at Kaskaskia, and when he received the letter from General Wilkinson rquesting him to come to St. Louis for a new assignment, he was pleased. The letter was dated July 30, 1805. His orders were to embark as soon as possible to explore the upper Mississippi and locate its source. He was also to calm the fears of Indians about the American take-over and choose more sites suitable for military forts for protection of the Mississippi River valley. As soon as he was on the way upriver, he started his journal. The first evening he wrote this report:

"Sailed from my encampment near Saint Louis at 4 O'clock P.M. on Friday the 9th Augt. 1805, with one Sergt. two corporals and 17 privates in a Keel Boat 70 feet long; provisioned for four months. . . ."

Old Man River was not very welcoming. On the first day, every person and many of the goods were soaked by a heavy rainstorm. The next day, after the baggage had been spread out to dry and the guns tested, they started out again, poling the boat. But the currents swirled about and the soldiers-turned-boatmen could make no progress until they got down into the water, took the cordelle over their shoulders, and dragged the keelboat up the river.

The bedraggled crew remained wet for the next three days, with not even a good catch of catfish to cheer them up. Rain or not, they averaged twenty-six miles a day until they had been on the river almost a week.

Old Man River tried another of his tricks on August 16—holding the keelboat in place on a hidden snag, as the tree limbs in the water were called.

"Saw it off," Pike ordered, and the unhappy, muscle-sore men plunged into the water to cut through the limb on which they were stuck.

The keelboat had a mast and a square sail, and some days the breeze was with them. One of those days was Saturday, August 17, when they made thirty-nine miles. But then came real trouble. On Monday they were going along fine until nine o'clock in the morning. Suddenly there was an awful screeching, scraping sound. This time it was a "sawyer," an underwater snag that moves up and down.

They passed on over it, but a little while later one of the men cried out, "We're taking on water!" It looked as if the boat would sink as water rushed in through a hole ripped by the snag. While some of the men bailed out water, others got the boat to the shore and unloaded most of the cargo. Then, with all their strength, the men pulled and pushed until the keel was on a sandbar and the broken plank was above water. A new board was fitted into its place and caulked with oakum.

The Pike expedition continued up the Great River. Sometimes Indians came to visit the camps. Pike would tell them about Governor Wilkinson "their father at St. Louis," who wanted to meet them, trade with them, and help them. Then he gave the Indians gifts of tobacco, knives, and whiskey, and after dark he moved his expedition several miles on before making camp.

The Des Moines Rapids, eleven miles long and just above the mouth of the Des Moines River, gave them another lesson in handling the keelboat as they worked to avoid wreckage on the rocks. The rapids were caused by a drop in riverbed level, as well as by the rock formations. Getting the boat up over the rises without overturning it was almost impossible for the men until they were helped by some experienced boatmen—Indians and their American government Indian agent.

Pike was not feeling well on September 1, already finding the life of an explorer very difficult. He ordered the boats pulled to the west bank, near the house of a Julien Dubuque and close to the site of present-day Dubuque, Iowa. Dubuque was a fur trader who had seen an opportunity to make money mining and selling lead smelted from the ore found around the Galena River (then known as Fever River) in northwestern Illinois, southern Wisconsin, and also on the Iowa side of the Mississippi.

The French had discovered that ore many years ago by following clues from the Indians, and some had mined enough to get supplies for making bullets. But Dubuque was the first to make a business of directing the Indians in mining it and shaping it into seventy pound "pigs." He had met the Indians in council and made friends with them, a friendship that lasted through years of their working together, beginning in 1788. Dubuque was polite, but did not offer to show the Americans the mines that were being worked, about six miles up the Fever River. He invited Pike to dinner, and introduced him to an Indian chief who, Pike wrote in his journal, made "a very flowery speech . . . which I returned in a few words, accompanied by a small present."

Of course, since he was supposed to report on mineral deposits, Pike asked many questions. Dubuque was careful about what he said because his lead mining operation east of the Mississippi was illegal. The Sauk and Fox tribes who worked for him there signed a treaty with the United States government in 1804, giving up their rights to that land. Dubuque's land, on the Iowa side, was about 500 square miles.

As Pike's men continued up the Mississippi, there were bluffs along both riverbanks. Just before they reached Prairie du Chien, an old French trading post on the Wisconsin side of the river, Pike saw the ideal place for a

THE MISSISSIPPI AT THE CONFLUENCE WITH THE WISCONSIN RIVER, AS IT APPEARS FROM "PIKE'S PEAK," IOWA. Contemporary photo by the author

government fort. It was on a high, broad bluff on the west side.

"A Spring in the rear, level on top, and the View of all the Country immediately under your feet," Pike wrote in his journal for September 5. He could see clearly the many islands in the broad Mississippi and, just to the left, the Wisconsin River blending into the Mississippi. To this day, that bluff is called "Pike's Peak"—the same name as a Rocky Mountain peak in Colorado, named for Pike when he was on a later expedition.

Before Pike left Prairie du Chien, he was given helpful information about Indian affairs farther north, and a peace pipe to take with him so that he would be received

43

by the Indian chiefs as a friend. An interpreter and James Fraser, a young man who knew Indian ways well, offered to travel with him to help in Indian councils. Fraser told Pike that the Mississippi would get more and more difficult to navigate as they went on, and advised him to leave his seventy-foot keelboat and go on with four smaller boats. Autumn had come, with more rains and colder nights, and Pike knew that Wilkinson should have had him start northward in early summer—winter weather was coming.

On the 16th of September they entered Lake Pepin, twenty-two miles long. Pike had brought the sail from his keelboat along, and he mounted it on the largest of his boats. The wind had raised waves on the lake, but "my boat ploughed the swells," Pike reported.

The Mississippi became much narrower when they left Lake Pepin. "I could easily cast a stone over the river," Pike wrote when they were approaching the Falls of St. Anthony. On Thursday, September 26, the entry in his journal began, "Embarked at the usual hour, and after very hard labour in getting through the rapids, arrived at the foot of the Falls about 3 or 4 O'Clock with my Boat— Unloaded her and got the principal part of the loading carried over the Portage. But the other Boat Encamped about 600 yards below, not being able to get over the last shoot full loaded. . . ."

The next day the second of Pike's two larger boats, which he called "barges," was finally hauled up the slope after it had slipped all the way back down on the first try. From the Falls of St. Anthony onward, as they tried to follow the Mississippi to its source, troubles multiplied. Winter snows, extreme cold, shortage of food and shelter—all added to Pike's problems. When men became ill, Pike saw that he must build a stockade and stop for a while.

On December 10, Pike and eleven others started upriver again, using sleds and canoes that the men dragged over ice and snow. It was almost impossible to even know for sure which way to go. There were times when they might have died of frostbite and starvation had it not been for help from men of some trading posts, still occupied by the British traders.

Because of the ice and snow, Pike could scarcely tell which of the many streams and lakes were part of the Mississippi. But on February 1 he stood on Leech Lake's frozen surface. That night he wrote in his journal: "I will not attempt to describe my feelings on the accomplishment of this voyage, this being the main source of the Mississippi. . . ."

He was not far from the right location, but others, searching in more favorable weather, would go farther. Pike had done his best against Old Man River's winter camouflage.

5

Upheaval
on the Mississippi

The Mississippi River was still a wild, lonely stretch of dark water when the Louisiana Purchase was made. The calls of waterfowl, the screech of an owl, the cry of a bobcat, or the howl of a wolf were often the only voices the boatmen heard from beyond their craft. They could go for days without seeing anyone on the riverbanks.

The only towns along the Mississippi below the mouth of the Ohio River before 1810 were those that grew from the small settlements around De Bienville's outposts— Natchez, Baton Rouge, and New Orleans. When a boatman was nearing the end of his five- to six-week-long voyage down the Ohio and the lower Mississippi, he was relieved to reach Natchez, knowing he had only about 370 more miles to journey's end. He was likely to make another brief stop at Baton Rouge, with about 240 miles to go. The only other signs of civilization were places where plantation owners had boat landings.

"Head 'er in!" and "Fasten bowlines!" were cries heard more and more often at the New Orleans waterfront after the port became American. Each year the number of boats tying at the docks increased, bringing loads of farm products, glassware, cast iron, and other manufactured goods down to New Orleans.

Most of the craft were flatboats from the upper Ohio, built of rough boards and rectangular in shape. These were broken up and sold for lumber at New Orleans. A few were the more costly keelboats that would also carry goods upriver. Many came all the way from Pittsburgh, but an increasing number, carrying mostly furs and lead, were from St. Louis and Ste. Genevieve, Missouri towns above the Ohio River mouth.

You can imagine how great it was for the boatmen to round that last bend and get ready to tie up at the New Orleans wharf. With money in their pockets from the sale of their goods, they were ready for a few days of celebration before starting for home.

By 1810, New Orleans had become the thriving seaport of which La Salle had dreamed. The city stretched nearly a mile along the river bank, with a levee ten to fifteen feet high and almost fifty feet wide to hold back rising river waters. Farmers, fishermen, and trades people used the broad top of the levee as a market place. About five steps down was the Place d'Armes (the open square) and the city streets.

47

The first log houses had been replaced after a fire swept through the city in 1788. An 1810 guidebook reported, "The houses in front of the town and for a square or two backwards are mostly of brick, covered [roofed] with slate or tile, and many of two stories. The remainder are of wood covered with shingles. . . . The population may be estimated at 10,000."

Quite a few Americans of all races had come to live in New Orleans along with the French and Spanish. The port city had become a busy center for the fur buying and shipping business, as well as for shipping the plantation products from the fertile river bottom lands.

Ships from the American cities on the east coast regularly made their way to the Gulf of Mexico. They entered the Mississippi delta and went up to New Orleans, a distance of about 108 miles. They mainly brought manufactured goods. From the Caribbean islands and Europe came other products wanted by Americans.

Some of the imported goods, plus sugar and cotton grown on the Louisiana plantations, were loaded onto the keelboats to be carried up the Mississippi. Most of the keelboats turned eastward at the mouth of the Ohio to go upriver to Cincinnati, Louisville, or as far as Pittsburgh.

Among the keelboat owners coming down the Ohio River from Pennsylvania and into the Mississippi in 1807 was a young man named Henry Miller Shreve, whose name would soon become well-known along the rivers. He was twenty-one years old and on his first voyage as proud owner and captain of his own small keelboat. Instead of turning southward to New Orleans, as all the other Pennsylvania boats had done, he headed upriver against the Mississippi current. Young Shreve intended to go to St. Louis to sell his cargo of Pittsburgh glass, hardware, and flour. He had heard that the people of the fur-trading village had need of these items.

His crew of robust men, in the traditional uniform of Ohio River boatmen—red flannel shirt and dark pants shrunken skin-tight from many dunkings in the river—had their first day of really hard labor as they turned up the Mississippi. Old Man River's currents were strong. Young Captain Shreve stood on the rounded roof of the cargo box, near the stern, handling the long steering arm and shouting orders to his men.

"Stand to your poles!" and three men on each side of the small keelboat took their places on the "running boards," the narrow cleated decking alongside the cargo box. "Set poles!" and each man had his long pole into the river. "Down on her!" and each was pushing with all his might and walking toward the stern of the boat. As the boat lunged forward, they turned about quickly and ran back to the starting point to repeat the action before the river could undo their progress.

When the current fought them successfully, they took the cordelle and went ashore. Sometimes they could "bushwhack"—running close to the bank and seizing bushes to pull the boat ahead. Whatever the method—warping, cordelling, poling, rowing, or bushwhacking—it was slow progress.

Three weeks had been spent coming to the Mississippi from Pittsburgh. Another three weeks passed before the small keelboat arrived at the village of St. Louis, then laid out in nine blocks along the riverfront and seven streets back from the river. No man-built levee was needed there, for docking was at a sloping waterfront that could protect the city from all but the most severe of floods.

Shreve sold his cargo at a good price and bought St. Louis' principal product, fine fur pelts packed in bales. These he took back to Pittsburgh. Since his was the first venture in importing furs via the Ohio River, he made a good profit on their sale to a merchant there, who in turn would send them by wagon to Philadelphia. From there they might even have been shipped to Europe, where the beaver pelts were especially wanted for manufacture into fashionable tall hats.

When he knew the needs and wants of St. Louis people and had become acquainted with leading citizens, Shreve knew exactly what cargo to carry there during the next years. He learned of Pike's visit with Dubuque and knew that the English Canadians had been buying most of the lead. At this time, tensions that led to the War of 1812 were growing between Americans and British, and the demand for lead was increasing as military build-up grew. Shreve saw that he would do well to go up to Dubuque's mines and buy lead for the American market.

When Shreve arrived, he found the Sauk and Fox Indians in mourning for Julien Dubuque, who had died a short time earlier. Shreve made friends with the Indians and arranged to purchase more lead "pigs" than he could carry in his keelboat. He bought a "mackinaw" boat, which is like a flatboat but pointed at both ends, that had probably belonged to Dubuque. With that, his keelboat, and a small flatboat his men built, Shreve was able to take sixty tons of lead down to New Orleans to sell at a good profit.

With those profits, Shreve bought a much larger keelboat, to carry enough cargo to be profitable for the New Orleans trade. But he was already interested in acquiring the newest type of boat—one that would make it unnecessary for men to labor so hard to get goods up the river—the steamboat.

In New York state, in 1807, a steamboat had been successfully put into service on the Hudson River. The owners, Chancellor Robert Livingston, politician and financier, and Robert Fulton, artist and inventor of the boat, had formed a partnership in steamboat building. Their object was to build steamboats for the Ohio and lower Mississippi Rivers, where the much faster and more efficient riverboats would be very profitable.

A steamboat named the *New Orleans* was under construction at Pittsburgh in 1810 when Captain Shreve arrived there. What a help steam power would be! He could make only one trip to New Orleans per season with his keelboat—five or six weeks downriver and twice as long to get back to Pittsburgh. With steam power he should be able to make three or four trips. Soon after his arrival, he bought shares in a steamboat being built in Brownsville, Pennsylvania.

Late in the fall of 1811, the completed *New Orleans* started down the Ohio River. She was still in the Ohio in December of 1811 when the worst earthquake in the history of North America struck.

The earthquake centered in New Madrid, a little settlement on the Missouri side of the Mississippi River about seventy miles by river below the mouth of the Ohio. There were three very strong shocks, the first at 2:00 A.M. on December 16, 1811, estimated by scientists today to have been of a magnitude of 8.6 on the Richter scale. Aftershocks followed this one, and people hoped it was over. But on January 23, 1812, another shock almost as severe as the first one came. The greatest shock occurred on February 7, estimated at 8.7. The shock waves traveled mainly eastward, and were so strong that church bells rang without a pull of the bell rope in Washington, D.C., and plaster on the walls cracked in Richmond, Virginia.

And what of Old Man River? As far as is known, never before nor since has he been in such great upheaval. In some places the riverbed was opened to view as the waters parted; for a while the river appeared to flow backward. The water turned red with the dirt from the disturbed river bed and the collapsing banks. Trees and great masses of land were torn from banks and islands.

The Old Man changed his course in so many places that part of Missouri went to Kentucky and part of Tennessee to Missouri. Reelfoot Lake in Kentucky was created where no lake had been—a permanent landmark souvenir of the New Madrid Earthquake.

Just before the first shock, John Bradbury, a British naturalist studying American plant life, was in St. Louis. He bought passage on a small keelboat with a French crew about to take a cargo of lead to New Orleans.

They reached the village of New Madrid on the evening of December 14, 1811. Bradbury kept a journal, and in it he remarked that New Madrid was "a disappointing place, with only a few straggling houses, situated around a plain of from two to three hundred acres in extent. There were only two stores, which are very indifferently furnished."

Little did Bradbury know that if he had come a week later there would have been even less of New Madrid to see! They left their mooring at the little village about nine o'clock in the morning on December 15. Their keelboat, faster than any flatboat, passed about thirteen of the cumbersome vessels taking farm produce down to New Orleans. The next night they were approaching a very difficult passage to navigate called "The Devil's Channel." They'd leave tackling that for daylight, and tied up to a tree on an island above the channel.

"After supper we went to sleep as usual," Bradbury wrote in his journal, "and in the night . . . I was awakened by so violent an agitation of the boat that it appeared in danger of upsetting." The French-speaking crew cried out, "*O mon Dieu! Monsieur Bradbury, qu'est qu'il y a?* (What can this be?)"

Bradbury hurried to the door of the cabin. The river was as never before seen. It was like a choppy sea, and there was a terrifying roar, the crashing of falling trees,

53

THE GREAT EARTHQUAKE ON THE MISSISSIPPI RIVER. Drawing, courtesy of The State Historical Society of Missouri

and the screaming of waterfowl. A moment later, slices of the island bank fell into the water and the boat heaved about uncontrolled.

He checked the time. It was 2:00 A.M. Not knowing what would happen, he gathered his valuable papers and money into a packet and went onto the island, carrying a candle. By its light he saw that the ground had split into a long chasm "not less than four feet in width, and the bank had sunk at least two feet." Before daylight, they counted twenty-seven lesser shocks.

When empty boats passed them they knew other people had not been as lucky as they. The tree to which their boat was tied was miraculously still standing. When they saw the "Devil's Channel" ahead, full of angry, foaming swirls and uprooted trees, the men were more fearful than ever. Somehow they made it through that morning, only to endure more violent shocks. They thought about going ashore, but the earth was rolling and unsteady with almost continuous aftershocks. Bradbury felt it was best to take a chance on going on down the river.

People reported bluffs splitting apart, holes opening suddenly in front of them as they walked, cabins shaken to the ground, and river water "thrown to the height of a tall tree." There were many reports of the ground suddenly caving in and sinking several feet. In the shock of February 7 the ground sank and left the townsite of New Madrid under water.

And what of the *New Orleans?* She shook and wove her way through the desolation. Just below New Madrid she tied up to a tree on an island for the night. In the morning the tree was still there but the remainder of the island was gone. The skillful pilot got the pioneer steamboat safely to New Orleans, arriving there on January 12, 1812.

The era that was about to begin was an upheaval on the Mississippi of another kind—the Steamboat Age on the rivers. It would bring undreamed of changes to Old Man River.

6

Steamboats and Guns on the Mississippi

There was great excitement along the Ohio and Mississippi Rivers when word came that the *New Orleans* had arrived safely in port. "Old Man River has met his master!" was said for the first time.

But he hadn't. The *New Orleans* was unable to return to Pittsburgh. The low pressure engine in the big blue steamboat was of a kind built to pump water out of a flooded mine, not to fight the Mississippi. In the Hudson River in New York where the Fulton boats were doing well, the engine did not have to move the boat against swirls and eddies and strong currents such as the Mississippi produced above Natchez.

On that first voyage, the pilot learned that the *New Orleans'* engine could not fight those currents successfully without risking explosion. The steamboat was caught in

56

swirling water when she approached Natchez, and for a while it was uncertain if she could make it to the landing. The safety valve on the boiler had to be opened to get enough power. From Natchez to New Orleans, the waters were deeper and the current weaker, much like the east coast rivers—there the *New Orleans* could do well.

Soon after the steamboat arrived in New Orleans, an ad in the newspaper announced that the boat would make an excursion seventeen miles downriver to the "English Turn" and back, a very exciting trip for those who were not afraid to ride on the noisy, fire-belching vessel. After that short demonstration voyage, the ads were for freight and passengers to go only as far up the Mississippi as Natchez. The *New Orleans* never attempted to go any farther upriver. Even so, business was so profitable that the Livingston-Fulton company immediately began construction of another steamboat at Pittsburgh, the *Vesuvius*—a good name for an early-day steamboat, for with full steam up, going against the current, the boat's stack erupted like a miniature volcano. This boat was to have a slightly stronger engine, but otherwise was similar to the pioneering *New Orleans*.

Captain Henry Shreve, headed back up the river with cargo for Pittsburgh in mid-July, 1814, was surprised to see the *New Orleans* close to the west shore two miles above Baton Rouge. He soon learned that because of the low water of summer the steamboat had become hung up on a stump during the night. The wooden hull was pierced and water had poured into the boat. Passengers and

57

freight had been taken off safely, but the historic steamboat had made her last voyage.

Shreve had seen an announcement in the New Orleans newspaper that the *Vesuvius* was leaving on June 26 to go all the way up to the Ohio River and on to Louisville. But the *Vesuvius* didn't make it to the Ohio in 1814. A short distance above Natchez, Shreve's boat passed her. The *Vesuvius* was held fast, hung up on a sandbar where she would have to remain until the autumn rains raised the river water level.

Shreve hurried on, for he wanted to complete this trip as rapidly as possible. The War of 1812 had been going on for two years and General Andrew Jackson had been ordered to New Orleans to prevent the British from capturing that very important seaport city. Captain Shreve expected to take command of the steamboat he had bought shares in, the *Enterprise,* as soon as he reached Brownsville. Then, he would load her at Pittsburgh with munitions Jackson had ordered.

On December 15 the *Enterprise* arrived in New Orleans. It had made the trip from Brownsville in two weeks, about one-third the time a keelboat took. The young captain, elated at the success of his first steamboat voyage, reported to General Jackson immediately. The General put the steamboat under martial law, and ordered Shreve to take her back up the river as soon as the cargo of munitions was unloaded. Shreve's orders were to bring downriver as fast as possible three keelboats, also loaded with munitions, that he had passed on his way to

THE *ENTERPRISE*, FIRST STEAMBOAT TO RETURN UP THE MIS-
SISSIPPI AND OHIO RIVERS TO PITTSBURGH. From an old drawing,
artist unknown

New Orleans. The *Enterprise* was the only operating
steamboat to help in the war effort because the *Vesuvius*
was again "hung up," this time at the New Orleans waterfront.

Having his steamboat under military law postponed a
problem Shreve knew he would have to face sooner or
later. He knew that under civil law, the Fulton-Livingston
representative in New Orleans would immediately serve
him with legal papers, or even bring a law officer to take
away his steamboat. The reason was that Robert Livingston had been able to get legal rights to stop all other
steamboat owners from using the waters of Louisiana,

which had just become a state instead of a territory. The Fulton-Livingston Company had a law passed to give them exclusive rights to travel by steam power on the waters of Louisiana. This monopoly would allow them to take possession of Shreve's boat, if they chose. They would at least prevent his loading freight and passengers for a return trip and make him pay a fine. If the lawyer Shreve had hired couldn't stop them, Shreve would be in big trouble.

Shreve and other western boatmen believed the rivers belonged to all the people and thought the monopoly was undemocratic. Other states and territories along the Ohio and the Mississippi had refused to grant such rights to Livingston and Fulton. But since most of the river traffic took cargo to New Orleans, the blockage of Louisiana waters was likely to stop any boat builder from investing in a steamboat. When he brought the *Enterprise* down the Mississippi, Shreve knew he was heading for a war of his own as well as the War of 1812.

The little *Enterprise* was very useful to General Jackson. He sent Shreve on many short voyages to take supplies to soldiers stationed away from the city. There were several trips fifty miles downriver to Fort St. Philip, where soldiers guarded the entrance to the river against the approach of enemy warships. Shreve also transported civilians to places of safety as the day of the Battle of New Orleans drew near.

When British ships came up from the Gulf of Mexico and were stationed south of New Orleans the *Enterprise* was called for a dangerous mission. Fort St. Philip desperately needed cannons that would fire a longer distance to stop enemy ships. The cannons and other supplies would have to be taken right past British guns guarding the river a short distance below New Orleans.

Shreve padded the sides of the wooden *Enterprise* with bales of cotton hung over the gunwales and waited until night and a heavy fog would help hide the steamboat. With the engine off they silently and safely passed the British ships. The return was more difficult because they couldn't get upriver without steam power. As they approached the enemy ships, Shreve ordered full power ahead. Even fog couldn't conceal the noisy, fire-belching *Enterprise* then. But the surprised British soldiers couldn't gauge their aim well enough and the bullets and cannonballs fell harmlessly ahead or aft of the steamboat. Shreve was hailed as a hero when he brought the *Enterprise* safely back to New Orleans.

The Battle of New Orleans took place five days later, on January 8, 1815. Captain Shreve bravely volunteered to man a gun to help guard the road just inside the levee, but his work with the *Enterprise* had been his biggest contribution to the American victory. Down at Fort St. Philip, the newly delivered cannons held more ships back. The Americans had control of the mouth of the Mississippi.

Old Man River must have been greatly disturbed by the gunfire and the cannonballs that fell into his muddy riverbed—the first time such things had dropped into his waters—but his shores remained American. Quiet returned to the riverbanks as the battle ended, save for the clanking and hissing of the *Enterprise*.

With the war—and martial law—ended, Shreve now had to face the legal battle to save the *Enterprise* from being taken by the Fulton-Livingston men. Shreve had the foresight when he was in New Orleans in the summer of 1814 to hire a lawyer, because he knew that sooner or later he was going to defy the monopoly. Robert Livingston had died in 1813, and Robert Fulton in February of 1815, but their company was not giving up on holding the use of the Mississippi for their own steamboats. Another of their steamboats, the *Aetna*, arrived in New Orleans while Shreve was waiting for the chance to head upriver.

With the lawyer's help, he was able to get the *Enterprise* released, but a suit was filed in court against Shreve. His lawyer would represent him, and Shreve could head back to Pennsylvania. However, he now knew that the *Enterprise* was going to have great difficulty getting very far above Natchez. If the spring rains came, she would stand a much better chance.

When May came, so did the rain! The Mississippi rose so high that the levees failed to hold the waters back and settlements were damaged. A newspaper reported, "The rise of the Mississippi has done great damage in Louisiana. Entire settlements were many feet under water on the 20th of May." Shreve and the *Enterprise* were well on their way in the Ohio River by then. He had solved his navigation problem by taking to the fields that were flooded, where the water was deep enough and the current not too strong.

In May of 1816, Shreve launched a brand new type of steamboat with many changes of his own invention. The *Washington* was as large as the Fulton boats, but it looked completely different, as well as having newly designed steam engines and other mechanical parts. The hull was built in Wheeling, in what is now West Virginia, by western boatbuilders who were accustomed to building keelboats. It was shaped to ride the Mississippi and Ohio Rivers. The boat looked top-heavy compared to the Fulton boats—it was the first of the double-decked, double-smokestacked steamboats.

The *Washington* was ready for a voyage to New Orleans, departing from Wheeling. But on June 7, just below Marietta, Ohio, a safety valve became blocked. There was an explosion and a sudden end to the voyage. This was a terrible setback, as it raised distrust of the high pressure engine Shreve had designed.

In September, when the problem was remedied and the repairs made, the *Washington* made a safe voyage to New Orleans in two weeks. There Fulton-Livingston men did their best to keep this fine new boat from returning to Louisville with freight and passengers, but Shreve's lawyer found legal loopholes and the *Washington* returned to Louisville without accident—*with* freight and passengers.

This marked the first steamboat voyage upriver from New Orleans to Louisville on the Ohio without accident, breakdown, or the aid of flood waters. It went down in history as the beginning of the Steamboat Age on the Mississippi River. Shreve made another successful voyage in the spring of 1817. "Old Man River has met his master!" was cried again and this time there was more truth to it.

Captain Henry Shreve did so well with the *Washington* that other boatbuilders copied his ideas—double decks, double stacks, high pressure engine, and more. In 1817, eight new steamboats were launched. That year the court in New Orleans finally made a decision that opened the Louisiana waters to steamboats of any make. With confidence, Shreve built two more steamboats, the *Ohio* and the *Napoleon*, both making their first voyages to New Orleans in 1819.

By 1823, the arrival of a steamboat at New Orleans was just an ordinary occurrence. It was that year that Shreve designed a steamboat with more passenger comfort in mind. He named it the *George Washington* and it was in service by 1825. The hull was flatter, and the boat required very little depth of channel. It provided the passengers with staterooms instead of two large cabins, one for men and one for women, as in earlier boats. Shreve bought the finest wood for trim and crystal for chandeliers. The *George Washington* set the pattern for the big "floating palace" steamboats to come. Soon others modeled after it were seen on the Ohio and lower Mississippi Rivers.

Not very many large steamboats went up to St. Louis at first. About the time that Shreve finished his first *Wash-*

THE *WASHINGTON* RETURNS TO LOUISVILLE AFTER A SAFE JOURNEY TO NEW ORLEANS. Drawing by Lloyd Hawthorne

ington, a keelboat named the *Zebulon M. Pike* was fitted with a small steam engine and was the first steamboat to arrive at St. Louis. She was a little boat, a midget alongside such ships as the *Washington*, and had just one smokestack. Her captain had to keep his crew busy putting wood in the furnace to get up enough steam. And there never was enough power—the crew had to pole and row with all their strength to keep her moving. On August 2, six weeks after the *Pike* left Louisville, the people of St. Louis heard her coming. A newspaper reporter wrote:

"The inhabitants of the village gathered on the bank to welcome the novel visitor. Among them was a group of Indians. As the boat approached, the

65

glare from the furnace, and the volume of murky smoke filled the Indians with dismay. They fled to the high ground in the rear of the village."

A steamboat that arrived in St. Louis in 1819, the *Western Engineer*, was planned especially to frighten the Indians. It was built to look as if a dragon were riding on the boat, with flame and smoke coming from its mouth. The stern paddle wheel was covered and painted to look like the dragon's tail, and it seemed to lash about as the wheel churned up the water. This steamboat was built to go up the Missouri River, and went as far as Council Bluffs, a new record. The next year, 1820, the *Western Engineer* went up the Mississippi as far as the Des Moines Rapids, but had great difficulty there and turned back.

By 1823, except in the coldest part of the year when there was ice in the river, steamboats docked at St. Louis and embarked every day. All of them were either small, very shallow draft boats prepared to go up the Missouri River for the fur trade, or huge sidewheelers getting ready to take passengers and cargoes of furs, lead, rope, and some agricultural products down to New Orleans.

But no steamboat had ventured any farther up the Mississippi than the foot of the Des Moines Rapids for fear of wrecking the steamboat on the rocks in shallow water. For all of the middle and lower Mississippi, the Age of the Steamboat had truly arrived, and soon the upper river would also know steam power—with help from the United States Army Corps of Engineers.

7

Up the River to
Its Source

On April 21, 1823, an excitable, talkative fellow stood near the landing at the foot of Market Street in St. Louis awaiting the time to board the little steamboat, *Virginia*. As he mingled with the crowd he drew curious glances. His clothing marked him as a foreigner, and his speech was heavily accented. Now and then he burst into his native language, Italian. He was Giacomo Beltrami, exiled from Italy for political reasons and come to "see America." He may well have been the first tourist on the upper Mississippi River.

When he left Venice, Beltrami packed his most treasured belongings in two bags, grasped his fine red silk umbrella, and toured Europe before taking a ship from England to Philadelphia. After "seeing the sights" in the East, he boarded a steamboat to go down the Ohio from

Pittsburgh, planning to go to New Orleans, but making frequent stops along the way. At his last stop on the Ohio River, quite by chance he boarded the steamboat *Calhoun*, which turned up the Mississippi to go to St. Louis.

On board the *Calhoun* was Major Lawrence Taliaferro, Indian agent at Fort St. Anthony. Beltrami bombarded Taliaferro with questions about the great river and the lands and people to the north. The major's descriptions held Beltrami almost speechless for a short time— time in which he decided he would go with the major up to Fort St. Anthony (which became Fort Snelling in 1824). And so Beltrami disembarked with Taliaferro in St. Louis, ready for more adventure up the Mississippi.

The crowd at the docks was unusually excited because the *Virginia* was the first steamboat preparing to go all the way to the Falls of St. Anthony. She was a small sternwheeler, 118 feet long, about nineteen feet beam (width), and five feet deep. There was a small cabin, but no pilot house. The steering was done with a tiller at the stern to guide the rudder as on keelboats.

The captain anticipated problems going through the Des Moines Rapids and, farther north, through the Rock Islands Rapids. But they were starting upriver when the spring thaws and rains would bring high water, which would help get the steamboat over the rocks at the rapids. The *Virginia* was carrying a cargo of supplies for Fort St. Anthony as well as passengers.

The passengers included Chief Great Eagle of the Sauks. Governor William Clark had arranged for Great Eagle to be a passenger, although the Indians who had

come to St. Louis with their chief to discuss problems with
the governor would have to paddle their canoe back to
their homeland. A Kentucky family bound for the lead
mine country was also going as passengers. Beltrami, who
kept a record book, wrote that the family boarded "with
their arms and baggage, cats and dogs, hens and turkeys;
the children too have their own stock."

Beltrami was curious about Great Eagle, and he was
also amused and a bit amazed when on that first day out
the Indian shed the uncomfortable military uniform that
Clark had given him in favor of the scant covering he preferred.

Of course there were no woodcutters selling wood to
burn in steamboat engines in those early days on the upper
river. So when the supply was low, the *Virginia* tied up
at the bank while the crew went into the woods to chop
and cut. Beltrami saw these stops as an opportunity for
great adventure. He shouldered his rifle, draped pistols
and sword in his red Italian sash, and went ashore, watch-
ing furtively for any "savage" who might be lurking behind
a tree. He was often able to get meat for the boat's dinner
table. He was an expert marksman and game, including
wild turkey, was plentiful. One day he bagged a rattle-
snake and saved the skin for his collection of tourist sou-
venirs.

Great Eagle was not as easily amused. He and the pilot
had a disagreement when the chief pointed out the proper
river channel and the pilot ignored him, resulting in the
steamboat getting stuck on a sandbar and causing delay.
Great Eagle swam ashore and joined his Indian tribes-

men, who had been able to keep up with the slow moving steamboat. When Great Eagle came back for his possessions, Beltrami, whom the Indian liked, asked for and received as a souvenir a Sioux chief's scalp that Great Eagle had hung from the handle of his tomahawk.

The little steamboat reached the foot of the eleven-mile-long Des Moines Rapids, near the mouth of the Des Moines River where Keokuk, Iowa, is today, and began to fight her way through nine miles of rapids. She reached a point where she could go no further against the swirling current and had to ease her way back. The crew unloaded much of the cargo, carried it past the rapids, and re-loaded it when a lighter *Virginia* had made it through.

As they approached the Rock Island Rapids, the voyagers stopped at Fort Armstrong on the west bank, where Davenport, Iowa, is now. An officer and his men assisted in guiding the *Virginia* in this very difficult ascent of fourteen miles. Even with help she was very nearly wrecked.

After a stop at the lead mine country to allow the Kentucky family and all their livestock to disembark, the voyage continued. Now the riverbanks became more scenic. Beltrami's pen was "struck motionless" by the ever-increasing beauty.

They stopped at Fort Crawford, on the east bank, where the Mississippi was joined by the Wisconsin River, the place where Marquette and Joliet had entered the Mississippi. Beltrami wrote, "The hills disappear, the number of islands increases, the waters divide into various branches, and the bed of the river in some places extends to a breadth of nearly three miles . . ."

A small French settlement, Prairie du Chien, was just north of the Wisconsin River. Except for a few Indian villages, it was the last settlement the travelers would see before journey's end. The bluffs rose high on both sides of the Mississippi. Officially, the land was Indian Territory, except for small tracts where the Indians permitted the building of army posts through treaties arranged by Pike.

There were 200 miles more to go above Prairie du Chien. The boat was usually tied at night for safety reasons, but one night a great forest fire so lighted the river that they saved time by traveling nonstop. They knew they were nearing the end of the voyage when they entered Lake Pepin.

On May 10, 1823, the *Virginia* nosed her way into the Minnesota River. In spite of all the stops, she had taken only twenty days for the 700-mile voyage. She docked in the Minnesota under the bluff on which Fort St. Anthony was built. Beltrami wrote that when the steamboat began to blow off steam, the Indians who were visiting the fort "took to the woods, men, women, and children, with their blankets flying in the wind . . ."

When Beltrami learned that the Indians knew of another lake that they believed to be the river's source, an idea grew in his inquisitive mind. Perhaps he, Giacomo Beltrami, an exile from Europe, would settle the question for the Americans—he would be the one to find the true source of the Mississippi!

The *Virginia* was soon on her way back to St. Louis, but without Beltrami. Major Stephen H. Long of the

71

United States Army Corps of Engineers was on his way up the Mississippi, leading another exploring expedition. He would go up the Minnesota River to find its source, and then follow the Red River of the North from its source to Canada, mapping the routes.

"I seized the opportunity of asking permission to follow the major," Beltrami wrote, "simply in the character of a wanderer who had come thus far to see Indian lands and Indian people. They first set before me the sufferings, the dangers, etc., which I must encounter; but as I laughed at these childish terrors they saw . . . that the attempts were wholly in vain." When Long, who didn't want the tourist with him, told Beltrami it would cost a great deal, Beltrami produced enough to buy a good horse and all the needed supplies.

"Mr. Beltrami," Major Long wrote on July 9, "an Italian gentleman of the order of Noblemen, also joined our party as an amateur traveler."

On July 23 they reached Big Stone Lake, which, with a creek that runs into it, is the source of the Minnesota River. They crossed the divide and were soon in the valley of the Red River of the North.

On August 9 they were camping at Pembina (now in North Dakota close to the Canadian border) on land the United States and Great Britain both claimed. There was a British colony and trading post there, owned by the Scottish Earl of Selkirk. At Pembina, after many disagreements with Major Long, Beltrami left the expedition to seek the source of the Mississippi.

Long wrote, "Mr. Beltrami, our Italian companion,

FORT SNELLING AS IT APPEARED IN 1844. From a painting by J. C. Wilds

having taken offense at the party generally and being highly provoked at my objecting to his turning an Indian out of our Lodge, left the party in a very hasty and angry manner."

Long didn't know Beltrami had been planning this departure all along. Beltrami sold his horse, trading it for a mule and supplies, and hired an interpreter and two Chippewa Indians. They would go across land to a branch of the Red, now known as Red Lake River (Beltrami named it "Bloody River"), and follow it to Red Lake, which is on the divide. The Indians had hidden a canoe in which Beltrami and his men would all go upriver, except for the interpreter, who would return to Pembina with the mule.

"Bloody River" ran fast, with many rapids. Beltrami and the two Indians went on, with the Indians frequently portaging the canoe and paddling it expertly when the river allowed. When they had a brief skirmish with some

73

Sioux Indians, the two Chippewas deserted Beltrami. He was left alone in the wilderness—with the birch bark canoe, his luggage, and a paddle.

He wouldn't give up. He tried to paddle the canoe himself but it only went in circles, so he pulled it upriver with a buffalo hide thong, laughing and singing as he went along in spite of his troubles. When a thunderstorm was coming, he unpacked his red silk umbrella and propped it open over his baggage to keep it dry.

He was thus trudging along, waist deep in water and testing the depth with the paddle before going through deeper water, when he met two canoes of Chippewa Indians coming down "Bloody River" from Red Lake. They were astonished to see the happy traveler and "that great red skin" hiding a mysterious cargo.

"Good day, my friends!" Beltrami called cheerfully, and they approached, although with caution. Beltrami unpacked some gifts as a sign of friendship. One of the Indians, an old man, agreed to turn back with this strange fellow and paddle his canoe for him. After a night in which Beltrami shot a wolf in the dark and nearly scared the Indian to death, this guide also deserted his employer. But he first took Beltrami into Red Lake.

Alone again, Beltrami went up a small stream that ran into Red Lake from the south. He met more Indians, and hired one to portage his canoe across a little plain of rising ground. There he found several small lakes connected by streams, running southward. He named the last Lake Julia, and was sure he had found the true source of the

Mississippi—the "Julian Sources," as he called the little lakes.

Eventually, wearing skin clothing Indians had given him after an unfortunate encounter with a skunk—and still carrying his red silk umbrella—Beltrami was standing before Colonel Snelling at the fort, telling his tale.

The colonel listened patiently, but he was not excited. Disappointed, Beltrami went by keelboat to St. Louis and by steamboat the rest of the way to New Orleans. There he combined letters he had written into a book of his "American Pilgrimage," but it sold only a few copies. A discouraged Beltrami was finally allowed to return to Italy, where he died in 1855. In Minnesota, the county in which Red Lake is located and a nearby town are named for this pioneer tourist.

Nine years after Beltrami's adventures, Henry Rowe Schoolcraft, Indian agent and mineralogist, sought the lake to which Indians had long referred as "Lac la Biche," Elk Lake. He located the lake and gave it a new name from a Latin phrase, *veritas caput*, which means "true head." Put the two words together and you see ver*ITASCA*put. And so Lake Itasca was named.

Although they had no instruments to measure the altitude, the Indians had long known how to find the source of the great Mississippi River. Now many people go to see it and wade across the Mississippi, if they so choose, in Itasca State Park.

8

Engineers Go
Up the Mississippi

When the United States took possession of Old Man River, the Army, under the direction of the Secretary of War, already had a working division that still exists today under the Department of Defense. Known as the Army Corps of Engineers, it was and is chief caretaker of Old Man River.

In the early 1800s, a major concern of the Secretary of War was protecting the people who used the Mississippi for transportation. A chain of forts was planned along its banks, much as La Salle had planned more than a century earlier. Officers of the Corps of Engineers—Lieutenant Pike, Major Long, and other officers—were sent with companies of soldiers to map the new American lands, to choose sites for forts, and to plan the construction. By 1824 there were United States Army posts from Fort St.

Philip on the Mississippi Delta to Fort Snelling at the Falls of St. Anthony.

In 1824, the Supreme Court made a landmark decision that would have helped Captain Shreve in his problems with the Fulton-Livingston case. No longer, the Court decided, could one state control a river that ran through or between other states. Such rivers would be under Interstate Commerce laws. This ruling, of course, applied to the Mississippi.

Who would take responsibility for care of interstate rivers? The United States Army Corps of Engineers. Protecting the people had been the Corps' major task. Added to that now was the job of seeing that the rivers were navigable. And a major part of that job was clearing away the treacherous snags.

All the snags were dangerous. Many a keelboat, flatboat, and canoe had been wrecked by running against them. When the steamboats came, the snags caused an even bigger problem, for thousands of dollars in cargo and many lives could be lost if a steamboat was wrecked—and more were wrecked each year as the steamboat engines were improved and the boats went faster, traveling day and night. Here was work for the Corps of Engineers to tackle, as soon as Congress agreed to pay the bills.

It was mostly because of the need to get supplies safely to the many army posts along the rivers that Congress finally agreed to spend the money. The Secretary of War then advertised for steamboat captains to send in plans for some kind of workboat that could be used to tackle the job of clearing the rivers. Captain Shreve drew up a plan, but the job was assigned to another riverboat captain. Work started on the Ohio River, but all the money Congress had voted was quickly used up as the men labored to get rid of the huge planters.

Captain Shreve's *George Washington* and his other boats were doing very well when the Secretary of War wrote to him in 1826 asking him to take over the task of clearing the rivers. Shreve took on the challenge. He designed a double-hulled snag boat with a giant wheel mounted between the hulls, and a windlass to wind the heavy chains that would encircle the snags. A heavy iron-clad, wedge-shaped beam was fitted between the bows of the boats. Steam power turned the windlass and ran the boat forward to hit the tree trunk at full power with the iron-clad beam. Shreve was sure it would either break the trunk deep in the river, or pull it up, roots and all.

"It won't work! It will just upend the boat," said some of the other riverboat captains, and they asked Congress not to vote the funds to build it. Shreve's ideas had been laughed at before, and he was sure this idea was as good as his designs for steamboats had been. Congress agreed and the *Heliopolis* was approved, built, and declared ready for work in July of 1829. Shreve moved her down the Ohio, seeking a big planter snag on which to test the machinery.

He found one. It was "sixty feet long and three and a half in diameter, implanted twenty feet in the bed of the river," Shreve wrote later. With full steam power, the *Heliopolis* rammed her beam against that ancient tree. The boat shuddered, bucked, and then, with a screech,

SHREVE'S SNAG BOAT, DRAWN UNDER SHREVE'S DIRECTION,
1847. Lithograph by August A. Von Schmidt, St. Louis

the windlass began to turn. The huge trunk broke off deep in the river, too deep for any steamboat to touch it. It was done "with the greatest of ease," Shreve wrote. The windlass hauled the great log up and onto a saw table where it was cut into lengths that would float freely on down Old Man River.

In a short time the clean-up work on the Ohio River was finished. The *Heliopolis* entered the waters of the Mississippi on August 19, 1829.

Early the next year a newspaper reporter wrote: "Capt. Shreve has perfectly succeeded in rendering about 300 miles of river as harmless as a mill-pond . . ." Congress didn't take long to say yes when Shreve asked for funds to build another snag boat, the *Archimedes*. As

79

time went on, he added three more to the government's fleet.

After he had made the Mississippi much safer, Captain Shreve's work of snag clearance extended into tributary rivers. In 1832, he tackled a job in the Red River of Louisiana that others said was impossible to accomplish. There was a giant "raft" of driftwood, about 160 to 200 miles long, on which new trees were growing, blocking steamboat traffic to the army posts farther up the Red. The Red was the only water route from the Mississippi to Texas.

Shreve, who had seen the Great Raft when he was working on the *Enterprise* for General Jackson, was sure that with his new snag boat, the *Archimedes*, he could break up that mass of driftwood and open the flooded land to settlement and the river to transportation. He took a working crew and began a task that took five years to complete. In the summers, when it was too hot to work in the humid, swampy area, Shreve attended to other river problems, usually on the Mississippi.

In the meantime, settlers had been pushing farther and farther into the land bordering the upper Mississippi. By 1818, Illinois had enough people to become a state. Indians still occupied much of the land along the river, however, especially around the old lead mines and the Rock Island Rapids. There was gunfire on the upper Mississippi when the federal government sent troops to force all the Illinois Indians to cross the river into Wisconsin Territory (future Iowa).

Most of the Sauk and Fox tribes gave in and went to

the Iowa side of the Mississippi, but Chief Black Hawk of the Sauks refused to leave his home area around the Rock River. In 1832, in the Black Hawk War, the army forced him to surrender. The Indians agreed to move west of a fifty-mile-wide strip along the Iowa bank of the Mississippi, known as the "Black Hawk Purchase." Gallant Chief Black Hawk and his loyal followers moved to the area around Fort Des Moines, up the Des Moines River and unsettled except for the fort.

It wasn't long before eager pioneers were settling along the Mississippi in the Black Hawk Purchase as well as on the Illinois side. With very few Indian residents left, Illinois changed in 1818 from a territory to the twenty-first state of the Union. But fifteen years later the future states of Iowa, Minnesota, and Wisconsin were still territories, not ready for statehood. The land, especially around the headwaters of the Mississippi, was still almost uninhabited. Only Indians and a few white traders and lumberjacks lived there.

Even after the *Virginia's* voyage in 1823, steamboats were not often used for reaching the settlements along the upper Mississippi. The Des Moines and Rock Island Rapids still blocked the way. Most of the lead from the Galena area was still being taken downstream in flatboats and keelboats. Occasionally, even some of the keelboats were wrecked on the rapids. When Major Long was returning from the Falls of St. Anthony, the keelboat in which he was traveling was wrecked, emphasizing to that officer of the Corps of Engineers the need for something to be done to improve navigation.

In the summer of 1836, the Chief Engineer, General Charles Gratiot, called Captain Shreve to St. Louis. The Mississippi's currents were carrying a great deal of silt to the waterfront, building a sandbar that threatened to block steamboats from docking. General Gratiot wanted Shreve to plan how the Old Man could be forced to move his currents back to the St. Louis side, carrying away the silt, instead of cutting a new channel along the Illinois shore. Since steamboats had come to St. Louis, the city was growing rapidly, but all would be lost if Old Man River had his way.

Captain Shreve drew up a plan to save St. Louis. Men hired by the Corps would build a log and rock jetty out from the Illinois riverbank at a point above the upper end of an island north of the St. Louis riverfront, forcing the current toward the western bank.

Shreve had also been ordered to see what could be done at the Des Moines and Rock Island Rapids to make them passable for small steamboats. Before the water level dropped too low, he went upriver in a small government steamboat. The pilot made his way carefully through the Des Moines Rapids and on to the Rock Island Rapids. There Shreve transferred to a small boat in which he could study the rock formations and river depths. When he knew them well he charted a channel to be cut through them. It would require removing some of the rocks. He also recommended that steamboats be guided through by licensed pilots, since channel marker buoys would be dislodged by winter ice.

The little government steamboat then made the easy downriver trip to the Des Moines Rapids. Here the Mississippi River bed was different. It had a single, almost uniform layer of rock sloping downriver for eleven miles, making the water too shallow for steamboats unless the river was unusually full. Shreve decided that a channel ninety feet wide could be cut along the Iowa shore rather than through the hard rock.

Back in St. Louis, the captain wrote up his reports and drew charts to show his recommendations. It was too late in the season for any work to be started in 1836, and he returned to his other duties, including the Red River driftwood work. Chief Engineer Gratiot assigned a young lieutenant in the Corps, Robert E. Lee, to do the work as soon as possible.

Captain Shreve had sent boats and equipment for them, but Lee and his assistant, Lieutenant Montgomery Meigs, didn't arrive in St. Louis until August, 1837. Lee tried to improve on Shreve's plans for saving St. Louis, but found nothing better. After surveying that site, they also went upriver, intending to check the Rock Island Rapids first. But when they got to the Des Moines Rapids the water was so low that their small steamboat couldn't make it farther. It was firmly grounded on the rock shelf. Lee and Meigs used the steamboat as a headquarters office, going out to it in a skiff.

The need to cut a channel around the Des Moines Rapids was obvious by then, but Lee thought it should be away from shore, nearer the Illinois side. The two of-

ficers went up to Rock Island in a smaller boat and Lee
agreed that Shreve's recommendation for the upper rapids
was correct. Not knowing the winter conditions in the
river well, Lee wanted the channel marked with buoys,
despite Shreve's view that they'd be dislodged by ice—a
warning that proved to be correct.

It was 1838 when the improvements were actually
started. Even then, Old Man River interfered with having his rock bed broken out. The water was so high when
the men arrived at Keokuk in May that they had to wait
until the river had dropped to its summer level. Not nearly
as much was done as they expected when early ice and
snow stopped the work in mid-October.

The three projects turned out to be far more difficult
than Captain Lee had expected, and costs rose from thousands of dollars to millions. He found rock cutting and
removal very slow and worked out a way to use blasting
powder under water. (Dynamite was not invented until
1867.)

Lee set a tripod platform over the rock, drilled a hole
through one layer, put a halfpound of blasting powder into
a small tube, filled the rest of the tube with sand, and
forced the tube into the drilled hole. The explosion split
only the top layer of rock, and there were several more
layers to be removed. It took years to make the rapids
passable, even for small steamboats, but when it was done
they no longer had to plan their trips during the weeks of
high water.

The sandbar at St. Louis was threatening to reach the landing area when the jetty from the Illinois shore was finally completed in 1839. There were cheers for Captain Lee as the current washed back the sand from the city steamboat landing.

With all this work improving and easing river travel, settlers arrived in growing numbers to take up land claims. The Indians were pushed even farther west. And of all the lands along the Mississippi, only Minnesota remained too sparsely settled for statehood when 1850 came.

It was the heyday of the steamboat on the lower Mississippi, the busiest time yet known on inland waters. On the upper river, the traffic was lighter, but the busy days were coming as settlers rushed to claim the fertile lands where they could grow grains to feed America.

9

Full Steam Ahead!

Picture yourself on the levee at St. Louis early in May of 1849. Off to the south you see the black smoke of yet another steamboat wanting to find docking space, but the line is already at least half a mile long. The big white boats are angled in to make more space. You are told that about 2,500 dockings were registered last year, and this year there may be even more.

All around you there are people, carts, horses, stacks of bales, and boxes. Someone is shouting above the din, announcing the time for boarding on one of the boats, but you can scarcely make out the name of the vessel. And in the talk you hear the words, "Gold" and "California" and someone asking, "Where's the next boat for the Missouri River?" Another, arms loaded with bundles and luggage, looks frantically for the *Dr. Franklin*, an upper Mississippi steamboat.

Business is booming. St. Louis is the changing and

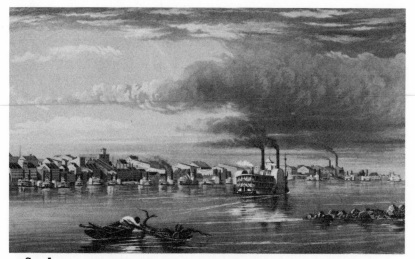

ST. LOUIS RIVERFRONT NOT LONG BEFORE THE 1849 FIRE. Courtesy of St. Louis Mercantile Library Association

Business is booming. St. Louis is the changing and shipping point for vessels going upriver, downriver, or to the east or west via the Ohio or the Missouri. The Gold Rush has added to the business tremendously. And yet, you know that there is trouble in the city, too. Every family, it seems, has lost someone to cholera, that dread disease that strikes babies and old people especially, but can lay low an able-bodied man or woman, as well. Some people blame the epidemic on the steamboat—it brings people that carry the disease, they say.

May 17, 1849, was a day of terror in St. Louis, one that would never be forgotten. It began as a lovely, late spring Thursday, bright with sunshine and a warm, gusty wind. As usual, a long line of steamboats was docked at the city's riverfront, decks almost touching the next in line.

87

And also as usual, the levee was crowded with people and goods. It seemed ordinary enough. And then, early in the afternoon, a dreaded call was heard. Someone on board the steamboat *White Cloud*, in the heart of the line at the dock, shouted, "FIRE!"

Flames shot up from the wooden decks of the *White Cloud*. Whipped along by the wind and the added hot draft from the burning timbers, the fire spread rapidly, seeming to leap from the decks of one steamboat to another. Before the volunteer fire department could get the "bucket brigade" started and the pumper manned, the flames were an unbroken sheet along the landing.

Each steamboat that had a crew on board was set adrift as quickly as the men could loosen the mooring lines and push the craft away from the levee, but twenty-three burned to the waterline within a half hour.

Firemen from every company in the city fought to stop the spreading flames, but soon a row of frame shacks above the levee was also ablaze. From them, sheets of fire reached out to the buildings along the riverfront street, mostly warehouses. Before the fire finally was under control, four hundred buildings and homes in fifteen city blocks were destroyed.

A few months later, the rubble was gone and rebuilding had begun. The levee was again stacked with freight, and steamboats lined up as if nothing had happened. This was a time in the story of the Mississippi River valley when people had "gold fever" or "land fever" and were heading west to the gold fields or the fertile plains. Most of the people and the supplies they needed came through St. Louis, the "Gateway to the West," brought that far by steamboat.

The finer steamboats had become more elegant as the years went by after Captain Shreve built his *George Washington*. But many of the boats were far from "elegant," and still without the privacy of staterooms. On them, the ladies had a small cabin at the stern, and the men a much larger one farther forward. All slept in bunks along the outer walls, some with curtains and some without. When mealtime came, the ladies were called into the gentlemen's cabin where a table had been set up in the long center space. A lady from England, Mrs. Frances Trollope, wrote of her steamboat experiences during a voyage up-river from New Orleans in 1827. She was disgusted with the manners of the American "gentlemen" at the table, for many used their knives instead of forks to get food into their mouths, and ate "voraciously," often talking with their mouths full. She also complained about their careless spitting of chewing tobacco.

But by the 1850s, the steamboats were more elaborate and the passengers perhaps more refined. By then the lower Mississippi boats were becoming "floating palaces," getting more and more elegant from then until the early 1870s. Mark Twain, in his *Life on the Mississippi* wrote of a typical steamboat:

"She is long and sharp and trim and pretty; she has two tall, fancy-topped chimneys, with a gilded device of some kind swung between them; a fanciful pilot-house, all glass and 'gingerbread,' perched on top of the 'texas' deck behind them; the paddle-boxes are gorgeous with a picture or with gilded rays above the boat's name; the boiler-deck, the hurricane-deck, and the texas deck are fenced and ornamented with clean white railings. . . ."

He wrote of how the black smoke could be seen before the steamboat rounded a point in the river, and a workman on the dock would shout, "S-t-e-a-m-boat a'comin'!" The levee would fill with people from every street near the river. They'd watch the boat approach, flag flying from the staff at the bow, the fires glowing through the open doors of the furnaces, and the deck railings lined with people. The bells clanged, steam hissed and men shouted as the steamboat nosed in to the landing. The "stage" was then lowered for the passengers who were leaving. Cargo unloading began after the baggage was taken to the carriages or "hacks" waiting on the levee.

Those who rode on the "floating palaces," if they could pay the fare, had small staterooms in which to sleep, rooms which to today's traveler would seem anything but "elegant." The staterooms were so small that two people would have great difficulty dressing at the same time. They dined in a carpeted area between the rows of staterooms, where tables were set with linen cloths and fine china, glassware, and silverware. The dinner was the main event of the day, with many courses, but some of the passengers found that it sounded better on the menu than it tasted in actuality.

PASSENGER PACKET WHEN THE STEAMBOAT ERA WAS AT ITS PEAK. Currier and Ives lithograph, 1855

Those who could not pay for such service were "deck passengers." When night came, they sprawled out wherever they could find space amidst the freight. When wood was to be taken on board, either from a "woodstop" along the bank or from a "woodboat"—a raft pulled alongside so that the boat could avoid having to dock—it was the duty of the deck passengers to carry the wood on board and stack it near the furnaces.

Towns sprouted along the Mississippi River in all but the lowest areas, where floods were a great threat. The largest new city to grow between New Orleans and St. Louis was Memphis, on a bluff where La Salle had located one of his forts. The city was incorporated in 1826 and grew rapidly as the steamboats became numerous. When the English lady, Mrs. Trollope, arrived there late in 1827, she was lodged in a new hotel, but had to reach it by struggling through mud on an unpaved path up from

91

the dock and along a newly marked off, very muddy street. Her shoes and gloves were "lost in the mire," she wrote.

The river towns all turned their faces to the waterfront, the artery of their life's blood. Besides bringing in goods and carrying to market the products of the countryside, the river also brought some fun into the peoples' lives. In those days there was little to amuse people. Entertainment came in the form of a special kind of riverboat—a showboat.

The first theater companies that arrived by river were known as "boat shows," instead of showboats. The show people lived on their boat, but they rented a place in each town to use as a theater—the largest hall they could find, often the courthouse. There the townspeople would fill the room to watch an act or two of a Shakespearean play such as *Hamlet,* or a short comedy or "melodrama."

The Chapman Players were one of the first boat show companies. It occurred to Mr. William Chapman in 1831 that it would save a great deal of trouble to have a boat large enough for a stage and an audience. He built a showboat, the first of many showboats on the rivers.

The first Chapman showboat was a flat barge, 120 feet long but quite narrow. A box-like building was erected on the barge, taking up most of the deck space. At the stern, there were wide double doors leading into the seating area, and at the forward end, a stage. The ceiling was very low above the entrance doors so that a balcony could be built above the doors for extra seating—backless benches. Behind the stage were dressing rooms for the actors, and beyond them, the living quarters.

The Chapman Floating Theater was a great success. It began entertaining people along the Ohio, but was soon heading all the way down the Mississippi to New Orleans. It was steered with a long pole to which a flat board was attached, poled along and helped by the downriver current. But when it came time to start back upriver, the boxy boat was too cumbersome. The shape of the boat had to be modified and steam power added.

It required a large boat to make room for all the people who wanted to see the show, however, and before long a showboat owner tried another idea. He bought a small steamboat with a good engine and put the theater in a flatboat. The steamboat pushed the theater boat from town to town. Someone would go ahead to put up posters about the shows that would be given and their approximate dates. The townspeople read the posters eagerly. By the time the showboat arrived at the town landing, there was a crowd awaiting the opening of the doors for every performance.

Probably the best known showboat was "Doc" Spalding's huge *Floating Palace*, on the rivers in the late 1850s. This showboat, pushed by a steamboat named the *James Raymond*, advertised plays and minstrel shows, but also a floating circus, complete with a trained bear and other animals.

We can imagine Old Man River being quite pleased that his waters were being used to bring fun and amusement to people. But changes were about to take place.

SPALDING'S *FLOATING PALACE*, AN EARLY POPULAR SHOW-
BOAT, LATE 1850'S. Drawing from an old advertisement

Railroad tracks had been creeping their way westward for
twenty-five years. City leaders in each town on the west
bank of the Mississippi talked of how a railroad to the
west should be laid starting in that particular town. It
would make the town a great city! Arguments were taking
place in Congress over United States' funds being used to
help build railroads to the new state of California.

In the early 1850s, railroad tracks were laid heading
westward from St. Louis and Hannibal, Missouri (the
town where young Samuel Clemens [Mark Twain] was
working in his brother's newspaper office), and from Davenport, Iowa, a town across from Rock Island, Illinois.
Work crews were extending the rails a little farther west
each day.

Tracks from Chicago arrived at Rock Island in 1854. But the "Iron Horse" had to stop at the east bank, and another "Iron Horse" would start out from the west bank when the tracks were laid. There were no bridges then, only ferry boats.

The talk among people was that soon railroads would take the place of the steamboats entirely—an idea that the people who worked on the riverboats did not like at all. There was an uproar among the steamboat captains when plans were afoot to build a bridge for the tracks to cross the river from Rock Island to Davenport. A bridge would stop the steamboats, with their tall stacks! Owners, captains, and pilots cried out against it.

The bridge building was not to be stopped. The Chicago, Rock Island, and Pacific Railroad had plans to build a bridge, cross Iowa, and then cross the Missouri River at Council Bluffs. The Illinois and Iowa legislatures authorized the Mississippi River span to cross from Rock Island to a government-owned fort on the opposite side, close to the new little town of Davenport.

The bridge was completed in April, 1856, and the steamboatmen were furious. While the bridge had been built high enough to clear most of the smoke stacks, the piers, they said, were placed in such a way that treacherous currents would cause their boats to be wrecked.

The bridge had just been completed when, on the night of May 4, the brand new steamboat *Effie Afton* approached it, bound upriver for St. Paul. She waited, along with several other steamboats, for the wind from the

95

northeast to die down, as two small steamboats had tried to approach the bridge against the wind and failed.

In the morning, two boats started toward the bridge, the *J. B. Carson* and the *Effie Afton*. The *Afton* passed the *Carson* and was approaching the bridge at good speed. The pilot on the *Carson* held back when he saw the river currents swirling around the stern of the *Afton* when she was halfway through the gap between the bridge piers. The new steamboat was driven against one stone pier and then the other, helpless in the whirlpools. A third bump against the pier on the starboard side finished the *Effie Afton*. On board, the passengers still in their berths were thrown out, and all were screaming. The boat was hung against the pier at a forty-five degree angle tilt.

Fortunately, the captain of the *Carson* was able to position his boat so that the *Afton's* passengers and crew could be rescued. But the troubles were not over. The heating stoves of the steamboat had been overturned and soon the boat was in flames. From below decks, the bawling of frightened cattle and horses could be heard. Then the wooden span of the bridge burst into flame. After a few minutes, the *Carson*, its decks crowded with *Afton* passengers, many only half dressed, cut loose and backed off to safety. The span of the bridge came crashing down upon the *Afton*, which spun downriver crazily, still aflame.

As the bridge fell, all the waiting steamboat captains rang the bells and blew the whistles on their craft. The steamboat had won the battle against the railroad!

Or so they thought. The railroad was not to be stopped. A new span for the bridge was built. The *Effie Afton's* captain sued the railroad company for the loss of his boat, a suit closely watched by every steamboatman on the Mississippi.

When the case came to trial in September, 1857, one of the lawyers for the railroad was Abraham Lincoln. River people were disappointed that the suit was moved to the courthouse in Chicago, where jurymen might have little understanding of the problems of steamboatmen. The speed at which the *Afton* approached the bridge was the factor that lost the case. The lanky attorney from Springfield also quoted figures of how many railroad freight and passenger cars had passed safely over the bridge in the new direction of travel—east-west instead of north-south. He successfully convinced the jury that the railroad had become more important than the steamboat.

The railroad and its bridges over the Mississippi had come to stay. The battle of steamboat versus railroad would continue a while longer, but the steamboat's heyday was ending.

10

Rafts and Gunboats on the Mississippi

Far to the north in the pine forests, men with sharp axes cut deep wedges into the trunks of centuries-old trees. As a tree swayed, the cry of "Timber!" rang out, then another tall pine crashed to the earth. Other men stood ready to chop the brushy small limbs from the long trunk of the fallen giant, while men with crosscut saws cut it into sixteen-foot lengths.

Teams of oxen dragged the great logs to one of the rivers that flowed toward the Mississippi—the Wisconsin, the Minnesota, the Chippewa, the Black, the St. Croix— any swift-flowing stream of the north woods. The logs were pushed into the river to float their way to a sawmill.

Some of the sawmills were on the tributary rivers, but the main ones were near the mouths of fast-flowing streams entering the Mississippi. The sawmills were usually powered with a waterwheel, turned by the flow of water over a dam. Whether the mill was large or small, very soon there were piles of logs awaiting cutting. After cutting there were heaps of sawdust, much of which made its way into the water—the first pollution from industry in the Mississippi valley.

Logging began as soon as treaties were signed with the Indians of Wisconsin and Minnesota, forcing the Native Americans into smaller areas called reservations. In Wisconsin, logging began in the 1830s after the Black Hawk War. The first government land office in Minnesota opened in 1848, the year that Wisconsin became a state. Immediately, there was a rush to buy the land. In 1851, millions of acres of land in western Minnesota and Iowa were ceded by the Sioux to the United States Government, and a new land rush was on.

Tracts thick with tall pine trees were bought by investors in the business of logging. They hired men, including many immigrants from northern European countries, who came west seeking "the land of opportunity." These men soon learned to swing an ax, handle a crosscut saw, or do any of the other labor of a "lumber jack."

The legend of Paul Bunyan and Babe, his great blue ox that measured "seven ax handles wide between the eyes," grew from those days in the lands where Old Man River had his headwaters. The tales were not written until the early 1900s, when the logging days had come to an end and the virgin forests were gone, but so immense was the industry that its fame spread throughout the United States.

99

In 1840 there were two sawmills on the Mississippi. In 1865 there were one hundred, many of them in river towns far south of the woodlands. The river became clogged with logs around the mills—the workers couldn't cut them into lumber fast enough. It took just forty years to cut away forests that had been growing for centuries.

It is difficult for people of today to understand how Americans of the mid-nineteenth century could give no thought to conserving the woodlands or keeping the waters of lakes and rivers free of pollution. Most Americans of that time saw the land as endless and the supply of nature's bounty as permanent, and were not disturbed. The loudest outcry came from steamboat captains who found that their boat engines were stalled by sawdust clogging the water intakes for the boilers.

After loose logs became a hazard in the rivers, logs were tied together into rafts so that they could be floated and steered downriver like a flatboat. A raft sixteen feet wide by thirty-two feet long would go down a smaller river to the Mississippi, where it could be tied to other rafts. A complete large raft might be 300 feet wide and 1,600 feet long, demanding very skillful handling to snake it around the many bends in the river. A crew of twenty-five to thirty men cooked their food and slept on the raft as they took it down the Mississippi to a mill.

People from Europe and the eastern states also came to the Minnesota frontier to buy land to clear, and before long they were growing wheat. Land could be had for $1.25 an acre, if a settler promised to build a dwelling and work the land. Near the Falls of St. Anthony, enterprising men built mills to grind the wheat. This led to the flour milling industry that started the city of Minneapolis.

By 1856, more than a million acres in Minnesota had been bought for settlement. Two years later, in 1858, the Territory of Minnesota became the thirty-second state of the Union. Now the entire course of the Mississippi River was within or between states—ten in all.

Steamboat traffic on the upper Mississippi had been increasing since the pioneering *Virginia* took supplies up to Fort Snelling. As immigrants arrived to settle the land, small steamboats took them up the Minnesota River and other Mississippi tributaries. Because the water was often not very deep in these streams, and because at times of low water it was still difficult to navigate the rapids in the Mississippi, the steamboats for the upper Mississippi were usually small stern-wheelers of very shallow draft. By the late 1860s, steamboats were used to push the huge log rafts downriver, much as barges are used today.

While the upper river valley was developing, the lower river was also seeing changes. St. Louis was growing rapidly. Among the new arrivals was a family with a son, James Buchanan Eads, whose name would become well-known along the Mississippi River. The Eads family arrived in St. Louis by steamboat from Indiana in 1833 when James was thirteen. Their last morning on the steamboat the dreaded shout, "Fire!" went up. They escaped with their lives and almost nothing else.

Young James, to help the family, clerked at a dry goods store for five years. His mind was far from the store most

of the time, however. Instead, it was busy planning the
building of a model steamboat or working out some mechanical invention. His interest in mechanics was fostered
by one of his employers, who had an engineering library.
The books Eads studied gave him the basics of an engineering education.

Every chance he got, James went down to the riverfront, which was just a few blocks from the dry goods
store, to see the steamboats arriving and embarking, or
loading and unloading. When he was eighteen, he deserted storekeeping permanently in favor of a life on the
Mississippi River.

His first job was as a purser, known on the river as a
"mud clerk," on an upper Mississippi lead trade boat.
He saw many steamboat wrecks, and knew that beneath
the dark waters lurked treasures on the sunken boats. His
inventive mind thought of a way he might make more
money by bringing up valuable salvage from the bottom
of the Mississippi. He designed a double-hulled boat,
something like Shreve's snag boat, but without the great
wheels and other equipment for handling snags. He
equipped his "submarine," as he called it, with hoisting
gear, pumps, and a diving bell.

Eads was able to get the boat built by offering a split
of profits to boatbuilders in St. Louis. For his first diving
bell, he used a forty-gallon whiskey barrel with one end
knocked out. He attached lead weights to the open end
and an air hose and cable from the boat above to the
closed end. With his head in the air chamber, he would
sink to the river bed or to a wreck and walk about. It was

dangerous work, but James Eads was a daring young man. Later, he wrote about walking underwater and searching the river below.

"My boat was held by a long anchor line . . . while I walked the bottom, under the bell, across the channel," he wrote. "The boat was then dropped twenty feet further down stream, and I then walked back again as she was hauled towards the other shore."

He never forgot how narrowly he missed death in 1851 when he was exploring the deepest part of the river sixty-five feet below the surface at flood time. One day, his boat was pulled loose by driftwood. Had he been on the bottom that day, his air supply would have been cut off and he would surely have drowned.

His daring instead brought him both wealth and a very close acquaintance with the riverbed. He learned first hand the science of hydraulics—the effect of water on the movement of solids. He noted the "scouring" action of currents in certain areas, the conditions that led to build-ups of silt in others, and what caused Old Man River to shift channels. This knowledge was of great importance to him when, in later years, he designed the famed "Eads Bridge" at St. Louis.

Eads was in poor health from so many hours in his diving bell when the Civil War began in 1861. Keeping the Mississippi River open was very important to the people of the North. Eads came out of retirement to put all his energy into a new project. He knew that the South was already adding fortifications to control the river and the port of New Orleans. The Union would need a river navy to open it, and he would build gunboats to help.

With his old energy back, he designed 600-ton "iron-clads" and got a government contract to build seven of them, agreeing to have them ready in sixty-five days. He and his former salvage partner started work at a shipyard at the south edge of St. Louis within two weeks of getting the contract. The first of their gunboats slid into the water after only forty-five days. Shortage of materials and an over-supply of "red tape" slowed the completion of some of the boats. But before long Eads' boats, were used in taking control of the western rivers north of Vicksburg, Mississippi.

When the Civil War began, all steamboats were immediately put under martial law. For the western states, the steamboat was the principal means of bringing soldiers to the military camps. By 1861, at least one hundred different steamboats were traveling the upper Mississippi all the way to St. Paul. On each trip southward, one or more companies would be on board, headed for a collection point at Keokuk, Iowa, or St. Louis. The steamboats also carried lead, shot, and gunpowder, packs of uniforms, and farm produce to supply the camps.

All along the Mississippi there were crowds awaiting the steamboats, cheering the enlisted men on. But a few months later, the steamboats had a much different reception when they began to bring home the wounded and the sick who had been discharged from duty. And there were many. Iowa alone sent 78,000 to war—half the able-bodied men in the state. Twelve thousand did not return

CIVIL WAR GUNBOATS SUCH AS EADS BUILT, IN A MISSISSIPPI RIVER BATTLE NEAR MEMPHIS. Illustration from *Harper's Monthly*

at all. Nearly 9,000 were wounded in battle and almost 10,000 were sent home because of ill health. All were taken to a river landing and journeyed homeward on the steamboats.

General Ulysses S. Grant used a steamboat as his headquarters for much of the time that he was directing the Union armies in the Mississippi River valley. He and navy Flagmaster A. H. Foote planned some very important strategies out on Old Man River. Among them was a plan to use gunboats in attacking Forts Henry and Donelson, on the Tennessee and Cumberland Rivers. This action, in February, 1862, opened the way for the Union Army into other southern areas.

Eads' gunboats and other steamboats were also used on the Mississippi River below St. Louis. With cooperation from soldiers on land, they took control of the southern fortifications in Arkansas, Tennessee (including Memphis), and nothern Mississippi.

At the same time that Grant was working southward on the Mississippi, Admiral Farragut was about to try to capture New Orleans by way of the Gulf of Mexico. The Mississippi River fifty miles below New Orleans was guarded by Confederate soldiers at Fort St. Philip on the east bank and Fort Jackson, a half mile downriver on the west. The Union military leaders decided that the attack on New Orleans should be made as soon as possible, before more Confederate troops were sent there.

In mid-April, 1862, Farragut entered the delta with six sailing ships and twelve gunboats, plus some schooners armed with cannons and a few steamboats to move the sailing ships where there was little wind.

Below the forts, the Confederates had placed a blockade made of old ship hulks chained together across the river. Farragut had this cut to open the way before they could make an attempt at "running" the forts. This they did, but not without a great deal of difficulty. The Confederate soldiers in Fort Jackson were ready for them by the time they had opened the blockade.

The "mortar boats"—those armed with cannons— bombarded Fort Jackson for two days, and were bombarded in return from the fort with cannon fire. When Farragut's flagship, the *Hartford*, tried to get past the fort, a "fire raft" was pushed against his ship. This was a raft on which stacks of oil-soaked wood were set afire. The fire spread onto the *Hartford*. With smoke billowing all around and sails aflame, the pumps and hoses were manned to try to put out the fires. Without stopping, the flotilla moved on upriver as best it could. To Farragut's relief, when the smoke cleared he saw they were beyond cannon range from Fort St. Philip and Fort Jackson, damaged but still afloat.

On toward New Orleans they went, meeting unmanned boats loaded with cotton bales deliberately set afire and floating down the river. These they dodged as best they could, only to meet a wall of burning ships at the New Orleans levee. Crippled as the Union forces were, they were still able to frighten the residents and what troops remained in the city into surrendering, and the battle was quickly won. Cut off from their supplies and support, the men at Forts Jackson and St. Philip also surrendered.

The Union generals realized that controlling the rest of the river was very important. It would divide the Confederacy, cutting off the states west of the river (Louisiana, Texas, and Arkansas), and weakening it in many ways. The Confederacy had been expecting help from France and England because of the Europeans' dependence on American cotton and other southern products. But when New Orleans fell, so did the Confederacy's hopes for this important help.

Although New Orleans was now in Union hands, the Mississippi was still not open from the north. There was a strong Confederate force at Vicksburg. After the capture of New Orleans, Farragut had unsuccessfully attacked Vicksburg from the river and had been forced to retreat southward. Now it was up to Grant to figure out a way to complete the opening of the river with as few losses as possible.

Under Spanish rule in 1790, there had been a fort built at Vicksburg on a bluff, two hundred feet above the river. When Farragut took New Orleans, General Grant was on the west side of the Mississippi River in northern Louisiana, about twenty miles north of Vicksburg. Grant reasoned that he would need to approach Vicksburg from the south—and, of course, on the other side of the river.

Grant would lose too many men if he tried to take his army downriver by boat. He decided he would go south of Vicksburg by land on the west side of the river, through Confederate territory, and have boats ready to ferry his men to the east side of the Mississippi. They would then go inland and come up the bluff from the east—the only direction that the bluff could be approached gradually. He would need the help of the navy to get his men across the Mississippi, of course.

There was also the problem of supplies for the men. Grant would have to risk sending gunboats and supply boats downriver, passing Vicksburg. With fires banked and engines stopped, the fleet made the move successfully under cover of darkness on the night of April 16, 1863. Again, on the night of April 22, six steamboats towed twelve barges loaded with hay, corn, and other provisions down the Mississippi.

Grant's men trudged through swamp, thick canebrakes, and tangled vines, heading south along the west bank of the Mississippi in northern Louisiana. Ships waited at the planned location, ready to ferry them across the Mississippi. After another long march, the Union troops took up siege positions surrounding Vicksburg, cutting off the approaches from all directions. Gunboats prevented escape via the Mississippi. It took a siege of forty-seven days to finally force the surrender of the Confederate troops on July 4, 1863.

The Mississippi was open to Union shipping once again. The end of the Civil War had not yet come, but so important was Old Man River that neither France nor England took sides with the South after they lost the river.

The Mississippi played another sad part in the Civil War. When peace finally came in April, 1865, there were many men held in the Andersonville prison camp in Georgia. They started for their home states by heading for Vicksburg. On April 24, the almost new and very large steamboat *Sultana* was waiting there to take on passengers. Repairs on a ruptured seam on a boiler had just been completed.

The steamboat had come up from New Orleans with only a few passengers. Now 1,000 soldiers at five dollars each would make up to Captain Mason for what so far had been a poor voyage. But many more than 1,000 soldiers boarded. When the *Sultana* pulled away from Vicksburg there were nearly 2,500 people on board, and her decks were groaning under the weight. Her legal capacity was 376.

Spirits were high among the soldiers, homeward bound at last. All seemed well until about 1:00 A.M. on April 27. Soon after the steamboat left Memphis, the midship section of the decks suddenly splintered as steam burst from an exploding boiler below. Many of the soldiers were sleeping and had no chance to save themselves. Only a few escaped by jumping into the river, grasping a section of deck to keep afloat, and being rescued when the wreckage floated back to Memphis. There were 1,647 lives lost in that explosion, the worst disaster in steamboat history.

Many other steamboats plied their way safely back to the home ports of thousands of other soldiers who had survived the agony of the war that scarred the nation. And not since then have gunboats been needed in the waters of Old Man River.

11

Change on the Mississippi

When the Mississippi was finally rid of battles and gun-fire, steamboats began to move freely again. At the war's end, steamboat owners still had confidence that they could win their war against the railroads. New steamboats were built, with more "gingerbread" and grandeur than ever.

The stories of the elegance of steamboat travel applied only to the cabin passengers. The deck passengers slept where they could, often in less comfort than the animals being shipped in pens on the lower deck. Their menu was different from that of the cabin passengers, and some-times, if they could, deck passengers went ashore and bought food while the boat was docked.

There were also differences in the quality of service and furnishings from one steamboat to another. The finest had good mattresses and feather pillows in the berths, while on a poorer steamboat the passengers might have to sleep on mattresses and pillows stuffed with cornshucks.

Pitchers of water and wash basins, with clean towels, were in each stateroom on the better boats. Other boats had but one washroom for men and another for women, and the men had to dip a basin in the river to get wash-water. On such a boat there was only one towel in the washroom. The story was told of a passenger on an upper Mississippi steamboat who complained that the towel was filthy. The purser replied, "Wal now, I reckon there's fifty passengers on board this boat, and they've all used that towel, and you're the first of 'em that's complained of it!"

The largest, best-equipped steamboats were on the New Orleans-to-St. Louis routes. These had a barber shop, a game room for the men (often with a resident gambler to make the card games more exciting), a music room for the ladies, and a steam calliope to provide cheerful sounds for all.

The captains of the finest steamboats took great pride in their vessels and the speed with which they could travel. Speed of a voyage was carefully recorded in hours and minutes as captains tried to beat the fastest time on record.

Steamboat captains often challenged each other to a race. If a captain observed a pair of gold-painted antlers on another boat, he was especially likely to offer to race, for if he won the race, his boat would be awarded the antlers, a symbol of superior speed.

It was in the year 1870 that two of these lower Mississippi steamboats, the *Natchez* and the *Robert E. Lee*, had the most famous of the many steamboat races that took place, one that set the all-time steamboat speed record for the distance from New Orleans to St. Louis. The race began at five o'clock Thursday evening, June 30, in New Orleans. There was an old rivalry between the two captains, John Cannon of the *Lee* and Thomas Leathers of the *Natchez*. The *Lee* had been built right after the war's end, in 1866, and was designed for speed and beauty. The *Natchez* was newer, built in 1869, and faster, according to Captain Cannon. That she was a fast boat there was no doubt. A good steamboat could go from New Orleans to St. Louis in four days, but the *Natchez* had, within the past month, made a trip to St. Louis that set a new record—three days, twenty-two hours, and nine minutes.

There were only a few passengers and no freight booked on the *Lee*, which had been stripped of shutters, doors, deck furniture—everything not needed to make the boat go. The deck near the coal-fired furnaces was stocked with things to make the fires burn hotter—barrels of fat bacon and stacks of pine knots, sticky with easily ignited resin. The *Natchez*'s captain had not gone to such extreme measures. He did have some freight and passengers, but fewer than usual because many people feared a boiler explosion when steamboats were racing.

The levee and the north wharf at New Orleans were crowded with thousands of watchers as five o'clock approached. The whistles blared, steam hissed, and bells rang. Now the huge side wheels began to turn, and the *Lee* backed slowly out into the river channel. Then, with

113

"A MIDNIGHT RACE ON THE MISSISSIPPI," AS NATHANIEL CURRIER AND JAMES IVES PICTURED IT IN THEIR 1870'S LITHOGRAPH.

a great groan, the paddle wheels reversed and she started upriver. The *Natchez,* seeming to be in less of a hurry, followed. Black smoke billowed from the stacks as they passed the official starting line.

At midnight, they were at Baton Rouge. The *Lee* was about nine miles ahead. There, and at all the river towns along the way large enough to have a telegraph office, the time of passing was recorded and sent on up the river. But then there is alarm on board the *Lee*—a steam pipe seam needs repairing. When the repair is made, the *Natchez* is only three minutes behind.

Captain Cannon had made arrangements for the *Pargoud,* a small steamboat, to bring one hundred cords of pine knots out to the *Lee* above Vicksburg to make the

114

fires extra hot. When the time came, all hands turned to transferring the wood while the *Pargoud* was lashed alongside. Both steamboats had to slow down from time to time to take on sacks of coal from barges alongside. Captain Leathers pulled to the wharf for a freight stop, but his slim, sleek steamboat made up for lost speed. The two boats were close when he, too, on July 3, had to stop to make repairs on his boilers. Captain Cannon added another advantage for the *Lee* when he took on two pilots who knew well the difficult stretch above the mouth of the Ohio.

In the early morning darkness of July 4, the *Robert E. Lee* was not far from St. Louis. Her stacks glowed with heat. As dawn came, many small boats followed her to glory. She approached the St. Louis riverfront and the cheers of waiting crowds rang out, joined by the clamor of bells and whistles from the victorious *Robert E. Lee*.

The officials recorded the time as 11:33 A.M. She had set a new record, and later it was engraved on the huge silver cup given to Captain Cannon—"Three days, eighteen hours, and thirteen minutes." The run was 1,278 miles.

The *Natchez* was skimming along close behind the *Lee* and might even have put on a final burst of speed and won. But a broken steam pipe and fog in a difficult part of the river, held her up. She stopped for five hours rather than hang up on a sandbar, and arrived in St. Louis on that long-remembered Fourth of July almost seven hours behind the *Lee*. Some said that Captain Cannon had broken rules by having a regular steamboat bring fuel. But, as others said, who could blame Captain Cannon for using his head?

As the 1800s were drawing to a close, so was the Steamboat Age. Fewer and fewer people rode the steamboats as railroad tracks formed a network to all parts of the United States. Shippers, too, tended to look to freight trains to carry the cargo that had been on the steamboats. A few showboats continued to travel the rivers from town to town, but even most of them soon found permanent dockage at large cities.

Mark Twain came back to St. Louis in the spring of 1882. He found it had grown and changed in many ways, "But the change of changes was on the 'levee,' " he wrote in *Life on the Mississippi*. ". . . Half a dozen sound-asleep steamboats where I used to see a solid mile of wide-awake ones! This was melancholy, this was woeful. . . . The towboat and the railroad had done their work, and done it well and completely."

The day was coming when Old Man River would be almost deserted, as city after city turned its back to him, preferring to face the railroad depot, grimy with soot from the noisy, smoke-and-cinder-belching Iron Horse.

With the Civil War over, railroad construction picked up where it had left off. A St. Louis editor agreed that technology was winning out because "rivers run only where nature pleases; railroads run wherever man pleases."

Although steamboatmen in St. Louis were against having a railroad bridge across the Mississippi built there, city fathers realized their city was losing business by not having one. Railroad lines planning to extend their tracks might converge at St. Louis if there was a bridge to carry trains across the river, to or from the city.

Chicago bridge builders were constructing bridges for three railroads going west from that city. The bridges were being built at Dubuque and Burlington, Iowa, and at Quincy, Illinois, helping Chicago's growth as a railroad shipping center. Chicago was beginning to call itself "Queen of the West," a title St. Louis had held for years.

St. Louis businessmen thought a railroad bridge would give St. Louis a chance to recover leadership. A call went out for bridge designs, and among those who responded was former river salvage man and gunboat builder (but never a bridge builder), James Buchanan Eads. One of the other competitors was the man whose bridge over the Gasconade River, west of St. Louis, had collapsed when the first train attempted to cross it. The danger of having that same man's design used at St. Louis spurred Eads on to draw up a design himself.

Engineers who looked at Eads' sketches thought his ideas preposterous. He planned a three-span arch supported by two shore abutments and two piers in the river. It was to be constructed of stone and tubular and flat steel, instead of the cast iron used commonly at that time. The arches would not conflict with the passage of steamboats, but would rise high above the Mississippi. There would be two decks. The lower one, for railroads, was extra wide to allow two of the new Pullman "Palace Parlor Cars" to pass each other. The upper deck was for wagons and carriages, with a sidewalk for pedestrians.

A CENTURY OF RIVER HISTORY—EADS BRIDGE, WITH THE
GATEWAY ARCH BEYOND, PHOTOGRAPHED FROM THE ILLINOIS
SHORE IN 1970. Photograph by Quinta Scott, for *The Eads Bridge*, published
by University of Missouri Press

Eads' design was accepted and work on sinking the
piers down to bedrock began in 1868. His personal ex-
perience in walking the river bottom helped him in the
engineering of this feat. The stonework for the supporting
construction at both ends began late in 1869. The bridge
between them was the final phase of the construction, completed in 1874 in time for a "grand opening" on the
Fourth of July, a day the thermometer hit 102°. The turn-
out was tremendous in spite of the heat.

It is remarkable that this beautiful bridge carried all
traffic across the Mississippi between St. Louis and East
St. Louis, Illinois, far into the automobile age of the twen-
tieth century. Now other bridges have been built for cars
and trucks, and the last train crossed this "milestone in
the history of engineering" when the bridge was one hun-

dred years old in 1974. The Eads Bridge served St. Louis and Old Man River well.

The bridge was not Eads' last service to Old Man River. While this monumental work was nearing completion, he was meeting with a Congressional committee at the Mississippi delta to decide what could be done for a problem there.

To get to New Orleans about one hundred miles from the Gulf, the ocean-going sailing ships had to come up through one of the three "passes" into which the Mississippi divides at its delta. The deepest one was the Southwest Pass, used by most of the nineteenth-century sailing ships.

The captains were advised in the 1814 edition of the *Navigator*, a boatmen's guidebook, "When in and bound up the river with a trading wind, run from point to point, taking care to keep out of the bends." It must have been a difficult job to navigate the distance from the sea, especially if the wind died. As soon as steamboats were available, a ship was helped up the pass by a small steamboat, acting much as a tugboat does in a harbor.

Even before the Civil War, ships were having a problem getting into the pass, or out of it into the Gulf, because Old Man River had been dumping silt where his current met the Gulf. He was building up soil just as the delta itself had been created. In 1859, one ship got stuck in the channel, leaving more than fifty frustrated ship captains waiting either to leave the Southwest Pass or enter it to go up to New Orleans.

The problem was brought before the Corps of Engineers and a survey of the entire Mississippi was ordered.

A great deal of dredging was done in the delta passes, but they seemed to refill almost as fast as they were dredged. With so little traffic during the Civil War, the blockage became worse. To the Corps, the only solution seemed to be to build a canal, which would be expensive to build and would require constant work to keep open.

When Eads met with the Congressional committee in 1873, he presented a plan he believed would gradually deepen the channel and prevent its refilling. He would build parallel jetties or dikes reaching far enough out into the Gulf to be in very deep water, where any silt build-up would not matter, and would be moved by deep sea currents anyway.

Only a few old friends backed Eads, men who knew that he was as well acquainted with Old Man River as anyone could be. Eads went before Congress the next February, but his ideas seemed about to be discarded in favor of the Corps of Engineers men who stood up to plead for funding for a canal. It was then that Eads startled them all. He offered to bet *ten million dollars* that he could open and maintain a twenty-eight-foot channel at the mouth of the Mississippi. After more scoffing from the Corps and complaints that the plan would just cause more problems, Congress accepted the bet and gave him permission to try—without funds from Congress until he succeeded. How could they lose? Even with so little risk, they made him agree to work in the South Pass, which was not as deep as the Southwest Pass.

When work began in June, 1875, observers were puzzled to see men cutting willow limbs on the mud flats of the delta, taking time out only to swat mosquitoes and wipe the sweat from their eyes. They then saw the men weave the willow twigs into mattresses. The finished pieces were weighted with stones and sunk to the bottom of the river along the banks.

Other workers appeared with loads of pine logs they had cut from the nearby woods. These were driven down into the water on top of the willow mattresses to form two walls. The man-made banks were extended well out into the Gulf.

Eads believed that natural laws would then cause the river to deepen—and he was right! In eight months, the newly directed current had deepened the eight foot channel to thirteen feet. By October, the channel measured twenty feet deep!

Progress was slow after that, and Eads had to do some dredging. Congress refused to pay until the depth was twenty-two feet. Eads was having to pay his men with promissory notes, but he kept on working. During the winter, he capped the jetties with huge concrete blocks.

There was illness and even death among his workers, and storms also caused delay, but four years after the work began, in July, 1879, the middle of the channel measured a depth of thirty feet at high tide. During the next year 840 ships used the South Pass. New Orleans again rose to leadership in American ports.

Later on, after paying Eads' bills for the South Pass deepening, Congress voted to have the Corps of Engineers use the same treatment (including the willow mattresses, which were also used for projects farther up the Mississippi) on the Southwest Pass, which again became the preferred entry from the Gulf.

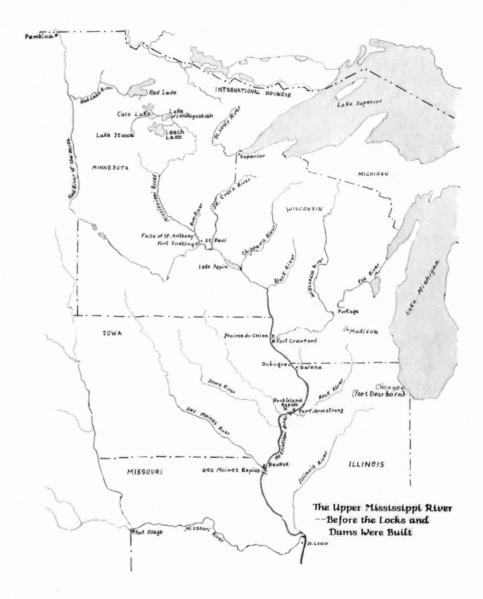

The Upper Mississippi River
--Before the Locks and
Dams Were Built

12

Engineers Take Command

The Steamboat Age may have been dying on the lower Mississippi in the 1870s, but it was far from dead on the upper river. The five states that the upper river flowed between were growing nearly half the farm products of the whole United States. And Old Man River, with his many arms, carried the produce to market. More and more steamboats were built for the upper Mississippi— 304 of them in 1866.

But there were still those old "bugaboos" in the river— the Rock Island and Des Moines Rapids.

Only small steam boats could pass them safely. In the Rock Island Rapids, there was a chain or series of connected rocks so famous for trouble-making that it had a special name—Campbell's Chain. It was named for Lieutenant John Campbell, in remembrance of his keelboat full of soldiers that was grounded on it in July, 1814, during the westernmost battle of the War of 1812. In this battle, Campbell's enemy was a band of Indians, fighting with the British against Americans. While the soldiers' keelboat was "hung up" on this great rock, the Indians attacked, killing sixteen and wounding twenty-one of the helpless men. Campbell was among the seriously wounded.

The rocks that form the Mississippi River bed at Rock Island and farther south at the mouth of the Des Moines River date back to the Ice Age, and are very hard. In 1867 the Corps of Engineers were ready to tackle the job of breaking them up.

To be able to work on Campbell's Chain, the workmen first had to build coffer dams. These were temporary low walls that blocked the flow of water. They were built by setting in two walls of logs, about ten feet apart, connecting them with iron rod, and then filling the spaces between the walls with clay and gravel pumped from the river bed.

The workers used an unusual method to break up the largest rock of Campbell's Chain. They laid huge piles of wood on it and set them afire. When the fire died down, they threw buckets of cold water on the embers. Presto—cracks in the rock at last! Then, with blasting powder placed in the cracks, they were able to break up the stubborn mass.

The deepening of the channel through the Rock Island Rapids cost much more than was budgeted. In one particularly hard rock area, two men worked for four days to drill a hole just twenty-three inches deep, dulling seventy-

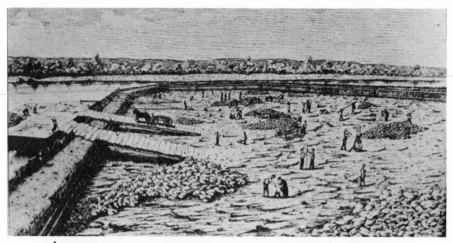

A COFFER DAM TO HOLD BACK THE RIVER WATER, UNDER CON-
STRUCTION WHEN WORK BEGAN AT ROCK ISLAND RAPIDS.

BREAKING UP CAMPBELL ROCK WITH FIRE. BUCKETS OF WA-
TER TO COOL THE ROCK RAPIDLY TO MAKE IT CRACK ARE AT
HAND. Both pictures courtesy of the U.S. Army Corps of Engineers

two expensive steel points. But the channel work deepened the water from thirty inches to at least four and one-half feet at low water, so that any steamboat could get through, even with cargo on board. In the long run the channel was considered well worth the money.

As the passages were made safe for steamboats, two river jobs became unnecessary. The experienced pilot hired to steer a boat safely through the rapids was no longer needed. Neither were workers who operated "lighters." Lighters were narrow flatboats, one hundred feet long by twenty feet wide. Horses walking along the bank pulled the lighter through the narrow band of shallow water between the bank and the rocks. A steamboat would be unloaded onto the lighter at whichever end of the rapids it was about to enter. This would allow the steamboat to rise higher in the water and gave it a better chance of getting through. The lighter would often reach the end of the rapids first, waiting while the pilot maneuvered the steamboat carefully through the passages.

The lighter crew made good wages in the days when a dollar bought a pair of leather shoes or a suit of woolen underwear. The charge was $1.00 per ton for downriver and $1.25 to "lighter" the goods upriver. This was expensive for the steamboat owner, who not only paid lighter fees but also paid his crew for a day of no work. With the pilot's fee, the cost of using a lighter would add up to an extra $500 or so.

While the Rock Island work was in progress, another crew arrived at Keokuk to try again to improve passage of the Des Moines Rapids. There the rock was even harder. The Corps of Engineers had already spent $335,000 on rock removal there before 1866, and only about 25,000 cubic yards of rock had been removed. A good part of that money was spent just trying to find a plan that would break up the rock.

The riverbed at the Des Moines Rapids was of solid rock with five gentle waves, continuing in a slope over eleven miles long. To cut a channel through the entire length would cost far too much. Years before, Henry Shreve had proposed a canal there along the Iowa side. This was the plan finally chosen, except that the canal would include locks.

There would be a wall built out in the river, twenty feet high and ten feet wide at the top, almost eight miles long. Upriver from this canal wall, the natural channel would be cut deeper and wider. Part of the riverbank would be cut away to make a good, six foot deep channel, 200 feet wide. There would be two locks to lift the boats, one at Keokuk and the other two and a half miles upriver. A guard lock, just above the upper lift lock, would be built first to hold back the water, while work was in progress, and later to catch debris. The locks of the canal would be eighty feet wide, 310 feet long and six feet deep. Thus began the building of the first lock and canal system in the Mississippi River.

Hammers struck sparks from hard rock, and drillbits smoked. Men worked to dig the canal with picks and shovels, and horses strained against the leather of the harness, dragging scoops behind them. When the digging was finished another wall was built on the land side. Little

127

by little, the walls were raised, the soil was moved, the canal took shape.

Railroad tracks had to be laid from the nearest quarry to the river to haul rock for crushing. Other rock, cut into blocks to build the canal walls, came from across the river where chunks were broken from a bluff on the Illinois side. For each of the three locks, a stone engine house was built to hold the steam engines that operated the pumps. Hydraulic pressure would open and close the gates, which were made of cedar and cypress wood—so sturdy that they didn't need repairing for twenty-five years.

More and more men were hired, and a "shanty town" was built to house them. During the first months there were 132 employees, but just before the canal was finished, ten years later, there were 1,600 on the job. People came by the hundreds to see this marvel of construction as it neared completion.

When the last section of the canal was nearly finished, the coffer dam sprang a leak, flooding the work. As soon as this was taken care of, an unusually heavy rainstorm raised the streams to flood stage and high water flooded the pit again. A strong current then washed away 600 feet of the coffer dam. But finally the job was done and the Des Moines Rapids Canal was opened on August 22, 1877. Bands played and spectators waved and cheered along the banks as the Corps of Engineers' sidewheeler *Montana* entered the guard lock.

This pioneering Mississippi River canal served for thirty-six years. The old canal was covered with fill dirt when the Keokuk and Hamilton Power Company Dam and Lock was completed in 1913. It is known as Lock and Dam No. 19. There is now a system of locks and dams between St. Louis and St. Paul, numbered from 1 where the Falls of St. Anthony once were to 26 just above St. Louis.

In the northern forests, the crews were still cutting away the big timber while the Corps of Engineers was working to improve the rapids passages. Lumber was the main product coming down the upper river after the Civil War. Every year, more than 400 million board feet of lumber—or the makings of it in logs—were rafted downriver. The peak years were between 1875 and 1915—the years that the river boats were fewer and fewer on the lower Mississippi.

Now the steamboat's whistle and clouds of black smoke hailed the coming of a great log raft, for no longer did the rafts float down steered only by men with poles. Each huge collection of log platforms was directed by a steamboat pushing it along.

At Winona, Minnesota, in 1878, 863 rafts passed under the new bridge. And still the peak hadn't come, for in the 1890s when it was obvious that the supply of pines large enough to cut was about to end, between 1,100 and 2,100 rafts came by—the larger number coming in years that the water level was high.

Old Man River was choking on sawdust in many places. The loud whine of saw blades passing through logs filled the air. The blades cut the lumber for the millions of frame houses being built, not only in the midwest but all over America. From the mouth of the Chippewa

LOG RAFT ON THE MISSISSIPPI. NOTE THE "BOW BOAT" THAT ASSISTS IN STEERING. From the collection of the Putnam Museum, Davenport, Iowa

River at the south end of Lake Pepin to St. Louis, the Mississippi flowed past seventy-three sawmills. They were sawing about 600 million board feet of lumber on a good day. It was the biggest business of the upper Mississippi valley.

When one of those huge rafts was approaching a bridge, great care in steering was needed. It became customary then for a large log raft to have another small steamboat attached sideways at the head of the raft. The idea was that this "bow boat" could force the raft to turn as it was drifting too far to either side, or maneuvering to enter a narrow channel.

It wasn't just the logging that kept the upper Mississippi busy. Immigrants had claimed farm lands and were raising wheat, which was milled with water power. On the west side of the Falls of St. Anthony, William D. Washburn built a thriving flour mill, and the city of Minneapolis grew around it. On the east side was the village of St. Anthony. St. Anthony and Minneapolis combined in 1872, and became the center for the flour milling industry. Below the Falls and the mouth of the Minnesota River, St. Paul developed as a business and shipping center.

Thanks to Old Man River, the upper Midwest had become the most productive part of the United States in tons shipped. Grain and grain products led the list, but there were also livestock, malt, wines, cement, and paper, plus manufactured goods.

The Corps of Engineers had converted old portage routes through Wisconsin and Illinois into river-canal systems to connect with the Mississippi. The ever-growing manufacturing and food processing plants of Chicago used the waterways even after railroads were complete. An important new manufactured product that was shipped via water from several river cities in Illinois was newly invented farm machinery—the horse-drawn reaper and other equipment that was cutting down the labor on farms. Along the Wisconsin and Minnesota Rivers there were paper mills shipping their production. Some iron found its way downriver from northern Minnesota. Cargo on the upper Mississippi even included the popular foot-powered pump organs for churches and homes, made in Illinois cities.

Through all this, the headwaters of the Mississippi still showed little difference from the days when Indians harvested the wild rice. Steamboats could not pass the Falls of St. Anthony, and when an experimental boat was moved into the river above the Falls, the work of getting it there seemed hardly worthwhile. The river was only deep enough for short spans, and was closed by ice for months of each year.

The Indians of the headwater lands who had not moved farther west lived on reservations, lands set aside for them by the government. They still depended on the wild rice that grew along the marshy parts of the Mississippi, and when the Engineers decided to build log dams in their reservation waters they knew their wild rice harvest would be ruined.

But the milling industry at Minneapolis wanted the flooding and water level changes controlled. Work was stopped by heavy spring floods; sometimes later in the same year the flow was so poor that the mills had to shut down again. The businessmen had much more influence than the Indians in Congress, so the dams were built at Lake Winnibigoshish, Leech Lake, and other locations to create reservoirs so that the Mississippi headwaters could keep the mills operating. The Indians lost to industry.

The Falls of St. Anthony were not the same as they had been when the explorers described them. They were breaking down naturally because the surface rock layer was thin limestone over softer sandstone. But the erosion

**THE FALLS OF ST. ANTHONY AT MINNEAPOLIS, BADLY DAM-
AGED AFTER MANY LARGE LOGS DROPPED OVER THE LEDGES.**
Photo courtesy of the U.S. Army Corps of Engineers

increased rapidly during the years when huge logs came
down the Mississippi from the sawmills. Great chunks of
the limestone collapsed. The Falls shifted back upriver
about 500 feet between 1857 and 1872.

The Corps of Engineers tried to slow the erosion by
building two dams above the Falls and a protective apron
over them. This didn't help much because this once beautiful span of the river was clogged with rocks and logs and
polluted with sawdust, mill waste material, and city sewage that flowed directly from drain pipes into the river.

133

Navigating the last two miles to St. Paul was very hazard-
ous. The Engineers decided to build a lock and dam
about a mile below the falls so that steamboats could reach
the "Twin Cities," as Minneapolis and St. Paul are
called.

In the meantime, the mill owners had been wanting to
use water power to generate electricity. Soon the Corps
began to plan a large dam and locks farther upriver, close
to the Falls. This dam would not just improve navigation,
but would also house generators in its interior. Construction of Dam No. 1, the first hydroelectric dam in the
United States, was completed in 1917, and nearly all
evidence of the Falls of St. Anthony disappeared. This
dam and lock system has been rebuilt several times over
the years, and is today known as the Ford Dam.

In the years toward the end of the nineteenth century,
as cities grew, steamboat transportation dwindled on the
entire length of the river, from the headwaters to the
mouth. Railroads carried more and more of the cargo.

Old Man River was left without much company for a
while, seeming almost useless. But he was far from dead!

13

The Mississippi, Alive Today

The virgin white pine forests were gone. The railroads were carrying much of the farm produce, and Old Man River was almost deserted, even on his upper reaches. Where there had been millions of tons of cargo shipped each year—lumber, produce, and manufactured goods— in 1916 less than one million tons went to market via riverboat.

On the lower Mississippi, a few of the floating palaces still moved from town to town bringing a brief glance at a fictional world to entertainment-hungry people. If your great-grandfather heard the sound of a lively tune played on the calliope drifting down the river, it could well have been from the *New Sensation*, a successful showboat operating from the late 1870s until 1907. Many of its plays were light comedies or popular melodramas. Some of the

THE *GORDON C. GREENE* ENTERING LOCK 11 AT DUBUQUE,
AUG. 24, 1948. State Historical Society of Iowa

floating theaters also combined mini-museums and circus acts with art exhibits, concerts, and plays.

The Bryant family of actors had a showboat going until 1942; it was among the last of the river-traveling troupes. The last showboat to tie up at New Orleans was the *Dixie Queen,* in 1940. St. Louis kept a floating theater named the *Goldenrod* docked at the riverfront the whole summer season. It was built in 1937 and was popular for many years.

A few passenger lines were still operating into the late 1920s. On the upper Mississippi the Diamond Jo Line worked out of St. Paul. On the lower Mississippi and Ohio Rivers, the most prominent line was Greene Line Steamers, managed by a famous woman captain, Mary (Ma) Greene.

The first great stock market crash happened in October of 1929, beginning the famed "Great Depression" of the '30s. Many college graduates, as well as untrained workers, were without jobs in those days, and every penny of each dollar had to go for necessities. There was little money for luxuries, such as an excursion on a steam boat.

All through the years of declining business on the upper Mississippi, rivermen and shippers alike had been urging a deepening of the channel to nine feet at low water time. This, they believed, would bring the towboats working on the lower river up to northern river ports and reduce shipping costs. Midwestern farmers would have a better chance to earn a living. It was costing all Americans more to get their food supplies from the farms of the midwest than to buy goods that came through the Panama Canal from the west coast—all because of the high cost of shipping produce by rail.

Senator Henrik Shipstead of Minnesota had been working hard for years to get Congress to vote for the nine-foot channel for the upper Mississippi. The barges could carry grain and many other products at far less cost, he argued, if only the towboats and barges could move freely on the upper Mississippi as they did on the lower river. A system of locks and dams would make this possible. When a river flows on sloping land, as the Mississippi does just below the Falls of St. Anthony, the depth of the water is changeable. Locks and dams can control the depth.

A dam is a wall built across a river, holding the water back and keeping it deep. Below the dam, the water level is much lower. For a boat to climb to the level of the "pool" held back by the dam, one or more lift locks are needed. The lift lock also serves as a lowering lock when the boat returns.

Each lock is a long concrete box with watertight gates at each end that can be opened or closed. On the low level, a boat enters the lock through an open gate. The gate closes behind it, and water flows or is pumped into the lock chamber. As the water level rises, so does the boat. When the level is even with the water into which the boat is headed, the gate at the upper end of the chamber opens, and the boat moves out into the higher level water.

The plan on the upper Mississippi was to build a "Stairway of Water" so that towboats, with their barges, or other river craft could go up or down that "stairway." It would be a series of 26 dams from St. Paul to just above St. Louis, lowering or raising boats 420 feet in a 669 mile length of the river.

The gates on all the new locks would be made of steel, electrically opened and closed. Water would enter the lock walls at the upper end through two tunnels with outlets into the compartment, filled by gravity flow. The water empties into the river below when the downriver gates are opened.

In 1930 Congress took the Senator's plea seriously and passed the Rivers and Harbors Act, which provided for building locks and dams as planned. Work began immediately on the nine-foot channel project. The Corps of Engineers hired thousands of men who badly needed jobs,

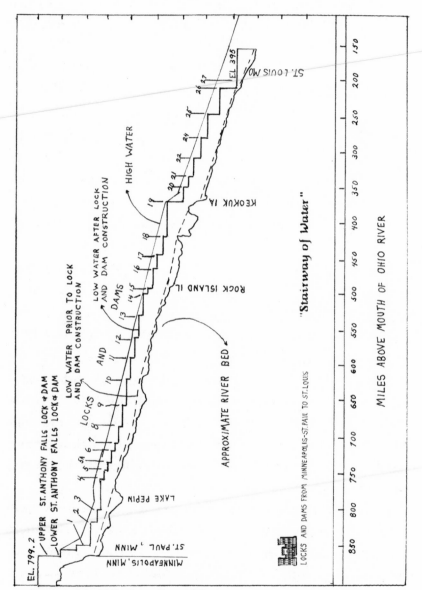

Courtesy of the U.S. Army Corps of Engineers

trusting that Congress would find a way to pay the bills. The Corps also ordered millions of dollars of equipment and supplies, which put factory employees back at work.

The uncertainty of meeting the bills still existed when Franklin Delano Roosevelt was elected President in November of 1932. The United States of America was still a nation of discouraged people, for many continued to be jobless. Roosevelt believed that the economy would get better if he created more jobs. He found ways for the United States to borrow the money, believing that was the only road to prosperity. The upper Mississippi project was included in his budget plans. The nine-foot channel work could continue. Old Man River had a new lease on life.

All involved in this tremendous work plunged into it as soon as joint planning had been completed. It was agreed that the locks would be as uniform in size as possible, generally 110 feet wide by 600 feet long. Models were built of most of the construction, and much planning had to go into the problem of what land would be under water at flood time and how the dams would affect the environment. To help solve these problems, the dams were constructed a little above towns to prevent flooding the town streets when the river level became too high. In ten years, a chain of 26 locks and dams was completed.

But the towboats could not make use of the new stairway up the Mississippi until terminals were built where towboats could load and unload, re-fuel and get needed repairs and supplies. When the terminals were built, some had grain elevators, or warehouses where goods ready for shipping were stored for transfer to the barges. A barge with a loading crane was also likely to be there. The cooks on board the towboats usually knew which terminals had the best fresh meat, fruits, and vegetables.

Soon the towboats were coming upriver. Some had a tow of more empties than cargo. The captains expected to bring farm products or even farm machinery down, or rolls of newsprint paper from the many paper mills of the north.

The standard size for a barge today is 195 feet long and 35 feet wide. One barge can carry 1,500 tons of coal or grain, or up to 10,000 barrels of chemicals or petroleum products. The tow might include barges for coal or chemicals, liquids or dry materials—each type of barge is planned for the cargo it will carry. Most are covered, but some are open. Many of the barges are rented from companies that specialize in a particular type.

The Mississippi towboats usually operate with a crew of seven or more, including a cook. A typical crew has a captain, a pilot, a chief engineer, an assistant engineer, a mate, a watchman, three deckhands and a cook. Often the cook is a woman, usually the only one on board.

Not all of the crew are on duty at the same time. They work in shifts six hours on and six hours off, around the clock. When a crew leaves the boat for time at home, it might be only for ten days while the towboat is getting ready for the next trip, or there might be two crews, taking turns for anywhere from two weeks on and two off, or thirty days on and thirty off. The tour of duty varies widely.

A GIANT SEVENTY-TWO BARGE TOW ON THE LOWER MISSIS-SIPPI. Courtesy of the U.S. Army Corps of Engineers

There is no special training school for towboat crews. Usually a person begins as a deckhand, "learns the ropes," and advances, taking tests for the more responsible positions that require a license.

In 1980, the freight passing through the locks totaled more than 34 million tons. One towboat with fourteen barges can carry as much freight as 140 steamboats could have carried a century earlier. The upper Mississippi is more lively than ever before.

The barge traffic continues in all but the months when ice blocks the way. There is competition among the tow-boat crews to be first to go through Lake Pepin and on to St. Paul each spring. In 1989, this was done on March 30, by the *Conti Nan*, with fourteen loaded barges. TV helicopters hovered overhead and cars lined the highway to watch as the barges pushed through. It was fourteen hours from the time the tow entered the lake until it left. Reporters wrote, "It is officially spring when the first tow goes across Lake Pepin . . . and the shipping season is officially opened."

Over the years, the Corps of Engineers has improved the harbors at some of the river ports. One at Dubuque, called Ice Harbor, is rectangular, and intended as a safe place for boats to spend the winter. It is situated away from the floating ice masses that often damage boats.

Other Corps projects have included completion of a system of six reservoirs on the Mississippi headwaters to control flooding and to keep enough flow for the Twin Cities area. Two dams were also built above the old site of the Falls of St. Anthony, and now it is hard to tell exactly where the falls once were.

The river banks where once Old Man River washed away great masses of soil have been reinforced with concrete. Jetties and levees, wing dams, and various other constructions have been built to control the current, the navigation channel, and the river's course in general. Some of the meander loops have been taken out of the lower Mississippi with cut-offs—sometimes with unexpected negative results, such as the formation of sandbars

THE PILOT HOUSE OF THE TOWBOAT *MELODY GOLDING* AND THE *JOHN C. BYRD* AT WORK. Courtesy Ole Man River Towing, Inc., Vicksburg, MS, Steve Golding, President

144

that blocked the mouth of a tributary river below the cut-off.

The cities grew fast along with Old Man River's traffic. But as they grew, pollution became a very real problem. For years, raw sewage and factory waste material were dumped into the river by most cities, from Minneapolis to New Orleans. In those days, people knew little about how river pollution could affect their health; their interest was in "commerce." Many were also using the Mississippi as a source of drinking water and knew little about water treatment. As disease spread, studies were made and steps taken to cut down on water pollution through water and sewage treatment plants, work that continues today.

Is the Mississippi River better because of all that has been done? Some people complain of what the Corps of Engineers has done to change the Old Man River, but a veteran pilot who has operated Corps boats for fifty-five years feels it is a better waterway today than when it was a wild river. This pilot worked both the lower and upper Mississippi. He remembers when the current changed from day to day. "You knew when you were out of the channel because the boat jumped like a bucking horse," he said for an interview. "You would come around a bend and see tons of soil sliding in the river after being undercut by the current. That was the Mississippi fifty years ago. It went where it wanted."

Now people like to remember the old days when steam power moved the big passenger boats. In recent years, diesel-powered excursion boats designed to look like the old steamboats, have been built to take people on short pleasure "cruises" on Old Man River. There are also some that are still propelled by paddle wheels. People love the leisurely riverboat cruises of three or more days on the boats with staterooms, a steam calliope, and many features to recall the old heyday of the steamboat.

If Old Man River could tell his story himself, he'd probably say he is pleased that people are finding pleasure on his waters. He might remind us that he can still cause trouble in spite of all the work of the Corps of Engineers. Above all, he'd maintain that he is definitely a living river!

THE FALLS OF ST. ANTHONY ARE SO ALTERED BY LOCKS AND DAMS THAT THEY SEEM TO HAVE DISAPPEARED ALTOGETHER.
Courtesy U.S. Army Corps of Engineers

Glossary of Terms

archaeologist—A person who seeks to recover and study, by scientific methods, the remains or evidence of ancient civilizations.

bank, left or right—The river's shores, designated left or right bank in the direction of the river's flow, as it would be to the person going downstream, never up the river. This is helpful on the meandering Mississippi, which changes direction often.

barge—In early days, a large keelboat. In modern times, a long, narrow, rectangular boat without an engine, designed to carry cargo. Left open or covered when the cargo should be kept dry.

beam—The breadth of a boat or ship at its widest point.

berth—A built-in bed on a boat; also, a space at a wharf for a boat or ship to dock.

bluff—A steep riverbank.

bow—The front section of a boat, rhymes with "how."

bowlines—The lines (ropes) attached at the bow.

bullboat—A primitive type of rivercraft, usually round in form, on a framework of slender, flexible tree limbs, covered with the hide of a bull bison.

bushwhacking—A method of pulling a keelboat upriver, especially when the water was at a high level and bushes could be reached from the deck. Each man in turn would seize a branch, hold onto it as he walked to the stern, and then quickly return to the bow to seize a branch farther upstream.

calliope—A musical instrument, fitted with steam whistles and played from a keyboard.

calumet—A long-stemmed ornamented smoking pipe, used in ceremonies by the Indians as a sign of peace. Also called a "peace pipe."

canal—A man-made substitute for a river; a water-filled ditch often built to connect one waterway with another.

canoe—A lightweight boat pointed at both ends, propelled by a paddle.

cargo—The freight carried on a boat.

caulking—Filling the spaces between boards of a wooden boat to make it watertight.

channel—The part of a river that is safest for boats to follow, as it is usually the deepest. In old days, it was cut by the river itself; in modern times, often established by engineers who build controlling walls, locks and dams.

cliff—Like a bluff, but higher and steeper and with a rock face.

coffer dam—A temporary dam built, usually of piled rock and earth, to enclose a space from which the water is pumped so that work can be done.

confluence—The place at which a river meets another river and joins it in the onward flow.

cordelle—From the French word for "rope," a term used to mean the long rope attached to a riverboat. As a verb, it means to pull the boat by means of such a long rope.

crew—Those hired to do the work of operating any boat, following the orders of the master (in command) and other officers.

cut-off—A new channel cut by the river current or by people across the narrow neck of land where a horse-shoe shaped meander loop has formed.

dam—A wall built in a river to hold back the flow of the water.

delta—An often swampy, triangle-shaped area of land at the mouth of a river, built up by the deposits of soil carried and dropped by the river as it meets the currents of a larger body of water.

disembark—To leave a boat on which you have been traveling. (See also *embark*.)

divide—The high ridge of land on which the direction of water flow divides, establishing the location of rivers. There are a few major North American divides, such as the Great Divide of the Rocky Mountains, and many lesser divides.

diving bell—A vessel or helmet-like covering, often bell-shaped, for people doing underwater work, open and weighted at the bottom and supplied with air pumped in at the top.

draft—The depth of a boat from the waterline to its keel, which indicates the depth of water needed to float the boat.

dugout—A type of canoe made by splitting a log lengthwise, shaping it, and then hollowing it, usually by a process of burning and then scraping away the charred wood.

embark—To go aboard a vessel at the start of a voyage, from the old name for a boat (bark).

falls—River water dropping as it passes over a cliff-like rock area in the riverbed, blocking navigation of the river.

flatboat—A boat built of beams and planks to form a rectangular box, often roofed over at the stern. A flatboat traveled mostly by means of the current of the river, and was steered with a long pole with a flat board attached that was used as a rudder. A flatboat could be moved upriver only with great difficulty because of its boxy shape.

glacier—A huge mass of slowly moving ice, formed by snow piled upon snow that did not completely melt during the year's warmest season.

gulf—A large area of a sea or ocean, partially enclosed by land, and often the body of water into which a river flows.

gunwale—The upper edge of a boat's sides, usually pronounced "gunnel."

headwaters—The upper end of a river, near its source.

hull—The main body of the boat, without the decks and cabins.

ironclad—A wooden boat with its hull covered with sheet iron for protection in wartime.

Iron Horse—A term used to mean a railroad locomotive, because the first railroad cars were pulled by horses.

jetty—A pier or other structure built out into the water to change the natural flow of the river.

keel—A beam running from bow to stern on a center line.

keelboat—A long, narrow boat, pointed at both ends, built on the keel, to which ribs were attached and covered with planks. A "cargo box" built for freight and passengers occupied a large part of the boat, but space was left for cleated "running boards" at both sides. Propelled upriver as well as down, by men using oars, poles, or the cordelle; sometimes also had a mast and sail.

levee—A built-up riverbank, usually of grass-covered earth and flat-topped, designed to hold back floodwaters.

lighter—On the rivers, a long, narrow boat pulled by a horse or mule walking along the bank, used to lighten the load of a larger boat trying to go upriver in a difficult passage.

lock—In a canal, the area enclosed by gates at each end to "lock" in the water or release it. The water level in a

lock is raised or lowered to lift or lower the boat to the next water level.

lockage—The process of entering and leaving a canal lock.

low pressure engine—A steamboat engine in which the amount of steam pressure that could safely be allowed to build up in the boiler (where water was heated to become steam) was not more than about forty or fifty pounds. The boiler for a "high pressure engine" could build up to one hundred pounds pressure, or even more, without risk of explosion, producing much greater power.

mackinaw—A boat similar to a flatboat but longer and narrower and pointed at both ends.

mast—The pole to which sails can be attached on a boat or ship.

master—On a steamboat, the officer in charge, usually the captain. Short for "master mariner."

meander—To make frequent turns rather than flow in an almost straight line. The loop a meandering river forms is often called a "meander," or "meander-loop."

monopoly—Complete control by one person or group of a product or a service.

mooring—The act of tying a boat fast, or a place provided at the river's edge for tying the boat's lines.

mortar boat—Equipped with muzzle-loading cannon.

mouth—The end of a river where it meets another body of water.

oakum—A mixture of fiber, such as hemp, with a sticky substance such as tar, used to make the seams in wooden boats watertight.

pier—In connection with a bridge, one of the supporting pillars.

pig—Lead, heated to a liquid and poured into a mold, hardened into a "pig," weighing about seventy pounds.

pilot—The officer who operates the steering device.

planter—A type of snag, often a whole tree, which has taken root or "planted" itself in the river bottom.

poling—On a keelboat, using a long pole by setting it into the river bottom, leaning against the padded upper end, and moving along the "running board" to propel the boat forward.

pool elevation—River level on the upper side of a dam, where the reservoir begins.

portage—The area of land between the waters of one river and another nearby that was crossed on foot by early travelers; also the act of carrying goods from one river to another, so named from the French verb *porter*, which means "to carry."

prow—The foremost part of a boat, usually pointed, rhymes with "how."

raft—A flat structure that floats, usually made of logs or planks tied together.

rapids—The part of a river where the flow is very fast, usually due to rocks in the riverbed along with a drop in elevation.

reservoir—The body of water stored when a dam is built in a river, often large enough to be called a lake.

right of deposit—The right of a boatman to unload his cargo at a port, for transfer to a ship to carry it to other ports.

rivulet—A very small stream of water that usually joins other large streams and eventually becomes part of a river.

rudder—The flat metal or wooden piece at the back of a boat to make it turn in the water, by means of a handle on the boat called a "tiller," or controlled by the pilot's wheel to which cables are attached.

running board—On a keelboat, a narrow strip of deck alongside the cabin, with cleats nailed to it to keep the men from slipping as they run back toward the stern while poling the boat.

sawyer—A snag which has an up and down motion in the water, like the arm of a person using a handsaw, especially treacherous because it was often hidden under the water.

scouring—Action of the current on the riverbed as it moves gravel rapidly.

shanty town—Quickly constructed low cost housing intended for temporary use of men working on a job.

showboat—A theater built on a rectangular boat hull, moved on the river by a steamboat, as the showboat had no paddle wheels or engine.

sidewheeler—a steamboat with a turning paddle wheel on each side, usually covered with a protective box.

snag—Any log, limb or even a whole tree in a river, the cause of many accidents when boat hulls were made of planks, as they were in the early steamboats.

snag boat—A steamboat, usually with twin hulls, used to clear the river of snags; equipped with machinery to raise snags from the river and saw them into short logs.

source—The flow of water where a river begins.

stage—In connection with a river, the level to which it has risen or dropped, such as flood stage. Also used to mean the walkway for passengers going ashore.

steamboat—A boat, propelled by the power of an engine in which the fuel is steam under pressure; designed for use in a river or lake, not out on the ocean where the usual double-deck design would not be safe in time of storm.

stern—The back part of a boat.

sternwheeler—A steamboat moved by a paddle wheel located at the stern.

tiller—A handle above the deck on a rod attached to a rudder below in the water, used to steer a boat without a pilot wheel.

tow—On the river, usually an assemblage of barges pushed by a towboat, usually powered by an engine that uses diesel fuel for power to turn propellers at the stern.

towboat—The boat, usually diesel-powered, that pushes today's barges. It does not actually *tow* the barges, since it is behind them and pushes.

tributary—A river that flows into a larger river is a tributary of the larger river.

voyageur—Many early fur traders on the rivers were French-Canadians and known as *voyageurs*, the French term for travelers.

ways—The structure, usually of wood, on which a ship or boat is built and from which it can be slid into the water when completed.

wharf—A place at which boats may tie up, load or unload.

windlass—A wheel that turns to wind rope or chain in order to lift or lower something to which the rope or chain is attached.

wing dam—A structure, usually built of willow mattresses and rock, either angling into the river to force the current to turn, or built on both sides of the river to deepen the channel.

156

INDEX